HOW NOT TO MAKE IT...
AND SUCCEED:
LIFE ON YOUR OWN TERMS

By

Anna Miller-Tiedeman, Ph.D.

Foreword by Lee Joyce Richmond, Ph.D.

Lifecareer and Career Compass are registered trademarks of the Lifecareer
Foundation

Library of Congress Catalog Number: 88-082957

Library of Congress Cataloging in Publication Data

Miller-Tiedeman, Anna
  How NOT to make it - and succeed.
  Bibliography p.
  Includes Index
1. Success. 2. Conduct of life. I. Title
BJ1611.2. M5 1989   158'.1   88-82957
ISBN   0-9613436-9-9

Terry Sherf - Editor
Cynthia Pietras - Production Assistant

First Printing 1986
Printed in the U.S.A.

Published by:

Lifecareer Foundation
993 "C" S. Santa Fe Av #180
Vista, CA 92083

To:

my mother and father,

Elmer and Pearl Miller

and

my husband and colleague,

David V. Tiedeman

And to *Life*: its wonderful forms and colors in humanity, in the earth, in plants, in animals, and insects; to the waves and particles in universe—all dancing together in patterned integrity.

Contents

PART I
LIFE-IS-CAREER™

6

PART II
LIVING LIFECAREER

PART III
OVERCOMING OBSTACLES TO
LIFECAREERING

8

**PART IV
TECHNIQUE AND LIFECAREER**

Foreword

In the body of career development literature, it's a rare book that addresses the needs of both the public and the professionals. *How NOT to Make it...And Succeed: Life on Your Own Terms,* is such a book. For the public, the book teaches how to reject the rejection that leaves us inert, whether the rejection is placed on us by others, or incorporated into the self. For the professional, it presents seeds of a new theoretical foundation leading to the practice of techniques through which we empower individuals to act in their own behalf rather than merely "help them."

How NOT to Make it...And Succeed, teaches clients and counselors alike that we are, each of us, powerful and wonderful persons living in a powerful and wonderful universe where *life works* for all of us all of the time because we are self-organizing systems. In brief, it illustrates how we are "in career," whatever we are doing, that the real world is wherever we may be, and that Lifecareer and the experience of it validates us as seekers, as knowers, and as high priests of our own destinies, and this regardless of color, creed, or culture.

Such a book does not require a long foreword. It speaks for itself turning words into actions even as it converts complex concepts into accessible energy. What does need mention, however, is the courage of its author, Anna Miller-Tiedeman because *How NOT to Make It...And Succeed,* offers new and scientific ideas, however poetically and mystically couched, to a field not inclined to mysticism, poetics, nor, unfortunately, to either science or change, though it would generally disclaim the latter.

When I first met Anna Miller-Tiedeman, it was as her roommate at the 1983 Assembly to Advance Career, convened in California by herself and her husband, David V. Tiedeman. Having arrived late and tired from the East Coast, I missed the beginning of the

Assembly, and when I couldn't immediately find the group and my place in it, I went to my room and slept. Hours later when I awoke, my, then unknown, roommate was there. The first words that Anna said to me were, "I'm here. I'm Anna, and I'll catch you up on things, but I'm glad you first had the chance to take care of your needs." She had, of course, provided a place for me to do just that. It seems to me that in this book, Dr. Miller-Tiedeman is extending the same invitation to all of her readers, whether the professional or the public at large, a place to take care of critical needs, an opportunity to "catch-up" on who we are, and space to be there with her on the growing edge of Lifecareer.

Lee J. Richmond, Ph.D.
Coordinator of Graduate
Programs in Guidance and
Counseling - Loyola College
Maryland, 1989

Preface

Why Lifecareer?

By the inch, it's a cinch. We all know that, but somehow we get bogged down into believing we have to put our precious energies into "making it"—often on someone else's terms—and usually in the work arena. Little attention is given to LIFE as a whole. We're told, "Now, listen up—if you want to make it, you've got to go to college. If you want to make it in business, you have to wear brown, black or gray suits. And for women, no frills or ruffles." All of this advice about the workworld, as though that were the only place to make it, or the only way to make it.

Meanwhile, we're busy living Life-as-career quite successfully. We lunch with friends, talk with our children, play Trivial Pursuit, follow our personal interests, work to keep ahead of the bill collectors, love, and just plain survive. And somehow each of us makes it on our own terms as we move inch by successful inch.

In living LIFE by the inch, however, some of us worry about how well we're doing (that's stress), and some of us measure what we're doing against what others are doing (that's more stress). But, some of us blessedly just plain don't care how we measure up—we're doing the best we can right now (that's Lifecareering).

In viewing our *Life* as our career, we can relax, realizing that we come into the world with our career and we leave with it. Our career is never lost. Having our career, we start looking for ways to support ourselves. We start by looking inward to see what we really care about and what feels right to us. At first, it isn't easy to know what we want because we have little work experience. We get that experience by working for other people. As we gain more and more experience in work and in life, we begin to get impressions of what we want to do next, even if it's only to take a frisbee break or eat an ice cream cone.

This isn't the usual message about career, however. Most of the messages we get while in schools and from the media regard career as a profession or a job. A recent article in the Careers section of *Forbes* magazine subtitled, "A Job, Yes; A Career, No," epitomizes the way we're encouraged to split our immediate action from our career. This article describes three college graduates who couldn't find work. One of them, a female 1982 Cornell graduate, couldn't land the job she wanted. She settled instead for a job in real estate. "However enjoyable a way station," she said, "it's not a career job." If she realized that *Life* is career, she'd regard her job not as a "way station," but as a part of her *Lifecareer* successfully unfolding in an equally interesting direction. That's the way *Life* works: if it's difficult to make contact one way, then make it another way. *Life* has all kinds of intriguing detours awaiting our exploration.

This woman's attitude typifies that of many college graduates. They play career like a crap shoot, hoping to beat the odds, land a "safe bet," and "make it." This approach can lead to disappointment. Just as doing what others tell you is their way to *success*? Why? Be–cause you're trusting almost exclusively someone else's information and not your own. Too, what any of us think holds only for the moment, even among people who think they know. Opinions change continually, so following what you feel is right in the moment is the best approach. For example, if it feels right to go on to college or graduate school, if you feel good about doing it, then what happens afterwards is inconsequential for now, because the journey itself is rewarding.

Sure, you want to find a job when you finish, but if you trust in the wisdom of doing what feels right now, today, then when you graduate, you'll know your next step. It may not be what you expect, but it'll be there for you. Why? Because you're using your Career Compass: your experience, intelligence, and intuition. You know that if things don't go right, they go left, and you also know that you won't be troubled or disappointed for long. As the Roman Philosopher Epictetus said in 82 B.C., **"People are not disturbed by things but by the view they take of things."** Therefore, take the view that *Life works*, not always the way you want it to, but it *works*.

As you continue to follow your Career Compass, you'll continue to make it—not on someone else's terms, but on your own. You'll know there are no "safe bets," only the here and now and the challenge. That's *Life*-as-career. And *Life*-as-career succeeds—it doesn't have to be "made."

If you regard job as career, you're in for much worry and stress because it's a perpetual competition—a "make-it" game. You're continually racing after something "out there," something you may—if you're lucky—catch. Peggy Holden, one of my former students, summed up an important difference between *Life*-as-career and Job as career: "Can you understand my *excitement* when I learned that a career was no longer something hazy that might be waiting in my future, but was the *present* I was living?" This book was written because I want you to know this principal truth: *Career is lived* not made. As my colleague and husband says, "Career is the path we leave behind."

Anna Miller-Tiedeman, Ph.D.

Acknowledgements

Special thanks to Leigh Wilson who worked with me to bring the *Lifecareer* spirit alive in playful ways, so it could be better perceived and understood. Leigh was always there, with lively ideas and a wonderful attitude. Even more important, Leigh lives *Life*-as-Career. He profoundly, experientially, intuitively, and intellectually understood what I was trying to convey.

Thanks, as well, to Ray Bradbury, who, as keynote speaker at the 1982 Santa Barbara Writers' Conference, inspired me to start this book. He said that an author should write about what (s)he loves instead of wasting time trying to learn what themes are popular. That was a turning point in my *Lifecareer*. I immediately took it to heart. Then Bradbury read his poem, *The Growing Into Me,* which begins:

> I will live
> If I live at all
> Not because anyone else,
> For I wonder if they did,
> But, because I knew me
> Or tried to know
> All the ways I tried to go

I'm grateful to Ray Bradbury: the spirit, the man, and his contributions to humanity.

While Leigh Wilson helped me convey the *Lifecareer* idea, and Ray Bradbury inspired me to start, Ms. Doe Chase helped my creativity with her deep tissue body work. In so doing, she freed up my mind, kept my body energies balanced, and helped me nurture and receive the ideas as they formed within.

Other contributors to this work were Marietta Battaglia-White, who first helped me organize the content, and Dr. Anita Mitchell, Dr. Lee Richmond,

Dr. Gerald Sankey, Gladys Sankey, Sharon Smith, Dr. Betty Bosdell, who read and made valuable comments on the manuscript.

Christopher Smith, a University of Southern California alumnus, and now a graduate student in Chemistry at the University of Chicago, checked the physics sections for accuracy. However, major conceptual leaps are my own responsibility.

A book comes about because of many people. I'm deeply grateful to all who gave me their help and support, including those who, when the going seemed difficult, gave me the spark and encouragement to press on.

Lastly, I'd like to express my deep appreciation to the following people:

Carol Lynch, Charles Fowler, Jean Goldberg, Jens Nowak, Marilyn Ravicz, Joseph Gardner Pillsbury, Marilyn Jesser, Nancy Knapp, Alex Gerber, Jr., Richard Carhart, Jessica Richmond, Lenore Lynch, Herman Williams, Sandy Olson, Valeria Roberts, Arthur Hitchcock, Keith Leafdale, Pam McClendon, Francis W. McKenzie, Barbara Gaughen, Allen Parker, Mike Obarski, Jerry Houser, Sharyn Slavin, Mary Mulvey, William Worth, Gilbert Wrenn, Kathleen Wrenn, Clayton DeLeon, Elizabeth Caulder, Richard Feller, Patricia Elenz-Martin, Naomi Larson, George Pfister, Tony Rose, Carol Rose, Jerry Lamothe, Gerald Olson, Jean Olson, Ann Grycz, Ann Tondow, Murray Tondow, Mary Malcolm, Peggy Van Pelt, Leatha Ann Martin, Cindy Miller, Dorothy Dallinger, Veronica Pottenger, Eugene Pottenger, Faye Campbell, Christel Skippon, Barbara Perrow, V. Cerese Massey, Clinton Smith, Sharon Smith, Donna Swanson, Merle Swanson, Mary Lue Zirkle, Paul Zirkle, Barbara Coffman, Carol Hershey, and Alan Hammond. I'm especially grateful to all the students with whom I've shared the *Lifecareer* concept at DeKalb (Ill.) High School, Northern Illinois University, the University of

Southern California, Johns Hopkins University, the Baltimore *Lifecareer* Connection Group: George S. Coviello, Harvey Huntley, Jr., Edith Picken, Edith Donohue, Barbara Horton, Lucy Wase, and Linda Kemp, Dundalk Community College, and Marshall University.

Copyright Acknowledgements

Appreciation to the following publishers and individuals who gave permission to reprint excerpts from chosen materials is gratefully acknowledged:

Gibran, K. *The Prophet.* (C) 1973. Random House, Inc., Alfred A. Knopf, Inc., 201 East 50th St., New York, NY 10022.

Roberts, J. *The God of Jane.* (C) 1979 by J. Roberts. Prentice-Hall, Inc., Englewood Cliffs, NJ 07632.

Keleman, S. *Living Your Dying.* (C) 1974 by S. Keleman. Random House, Inc., 201 E. 50th St., New York, NY 10022, and The Bookworks.

Gawain, S. *Creative Visualization.* (C) 1978 by S. Gawain. Whatever Publishing, Inc., Mill Valley, CA.

Bradbury, R. *Collected Poems.* (C) 1983. Lord Jim Press, Northridge, CA.

Marx-Hubbard, B. *The Evolutionary Journey.* (C) 1982 by B. Marx-Hubbard. Evolutionary Press, 2418 Clement Street, San Francisco, CA 94121.

Lifecareer Map

Lifecareer functions in a quantum universe which suggests everything is connected in a web of relationships. Therefore, several main ideas show up in various chapters to reinforce different ideas. This is due to their connectedness and interrelatedness. For instance, as shown below, the Career Compass idea is in Chapters 1, 6, 7, 15, and 16, and the classical and quantum physics ideas are in Chapters 2, 4, 5, 6, 7, 10, 11, 12, 13, and 14. The core Lifecareer ideas just have that degree of connectedness.

Chpt.	Career Compass	Create Your Own Reality	Left Not Wrong turns	Classical/ Quantum Physics	Cultural Shifts
1	✓	✓	✓		
2		✓	✓	✓	
3					
4		✓		✓	✓
5				✓	
6	✓	✓	✓	✓	
7	✓	✓	✓	✓	
8					
9		✓	✓		
10			✓	✓	
11		✓	✓	✓	✓
12			✓	✓	
13				✓	✓
14		✓		✓	✓
15	✓				✓
16	✓	✓			

PART I

LIFE-IS-CAREER

1

WHAT DO YOU MEAN, LIFE-IS-CAREER UNFOLDING?

Differences

Traditional career assumes job is career; Lifecareer assumes Life is career.

In the Beginning

In the beginning, *Life* was career, and people lived *Life-as-career* because that was natural.

Life in those days was finding something to eat, a place to sleep, fending off saber-tooth tigers, and washing one's loincloth. There was no distinction between *life* and career. Living was a full-time job. Then along came some Neanderthal, who said, "Hey, guys, help me bag this woolly mammoth and I'll give you its left forequarter." After that, people gradually began to think of *careers* as earning a living, a separate life function.

Slavery or servitude supplied the first *jobs* in which one person worked for another in return for a given amount of food and shelter. While the degree of servitude varied, being forced to work for another, without choice, is servitude.

Today things are different. The chains that bound slaves in earlier times have been replaced by other chains, often of our own making. The strongest chain of all is fear, and you'll learn in this book how to free yourself from it. Not only the fear of failure, but the even more intimidating fear of *they*.

"What will *they* think if I don't go to college?"

"Will *they* think I'm crazy if I refuse a good-paying job for a lesser one that's more interesting?"

"What will *they* say if I tell *them* I want to quit work and start my own business?"

The truth is that what *they* think or say really doesn't matter. When it *does* matter to you, it's because you've made it part of your reality. In this book, you'll learn that you do create your own reality and you'll learn how to make (or unmake) it. Remember: If what you do or don't do is based on *they*, you've forged your own chains. And you're making realities that can kill you.

You can even be self-employed and still be bound by self-made chains of servitude. If you don't like what you're doing for a living, it's *work*. But, if you enjoy what you're doing—if you've found your calling, that's *fullering*, and that's also what this book is about. You get a warm, good feeling when you're *fullering* because you're doing what you love. Or you're doing what feels right to you. Even if you don't love what you're doing, it may feel right because it'll lead to the next step. And when you love or feel right about what you're doing, chances are you'll make more money at it, too. This book also is about how to handle change, and if change weren't frightening, it'd be called something like *strawberries and whipped cream*, instead of *change*. Change and uncertainty are the only constants in the universe. How you deal with change determines how you live.

Jobs, occupations, and professions come and go and change. Your livelihood is only one piece of the puzzle, and not your entire life. *Life,* and all we put into it, is our career. Our eating time; our wash-our-socks time; our clean-the-house time; our ride-the-bus time; our paid-work time; our feel-good time; our get-sick time; everything we do in life is our career.

We All Live Life-As-Career

Maybe you don't think *you* live *Life*-as-career, but that's what we're all doing, because it's natural. We don't have to worry about *Life:* it continues to propel us forward. It's been working for billions of years, so we've learned we can trust it. That's another thing you'll learn in this book: that life is self organizing in your cells and in your *Lifecareer.* Life is a survivor. It'll be around even if we humans manage to destroy ourselves.

Some people knowingly live *Life*-as-career, and they get joy from watching it unfold. This doesn't mean they sit on their duffs and wait for great revelations. On the contrary, they fill each moment with what then seems right, and they watch how this activity begins to work for them. In this book you'll read about some of these people.

Many of these individuals find that what they need (not necessarily what they want) comes to them. They describe it as "I fell into it." Or "I got lucky," or "You won't believe it, but last week I needed $50.33 to pay my phone bill and that very morning I received a $50.00 tax refund in the mail." A student recently told me his motorcycle had stalled on the freeway. He rolled it up onto the shoulder. There, looking down, he spotted a Phillips screwdriver someone had dropped in the dirt—exactly what he needed to fix his motorcycle! You probably have had similar experiences. Some people call it a *stroke of luck*, while others call it a *stroke of the universe*, and still others say *the Lord took care of them*. In Star Wars lingo it'd be called *the Force*. However you describe it, most of you know you've experienced it sometime in your life.

Left is merely the other side of right, it's not wrong.

People who actively live *Life*-as-career believe that *Life* is about learning; there's no one, or right, way to solve problems. They know that right and left go together. Left is merely the other side of right—it's not wrong. Notice that you've got a right foot and a left foot, not a right foot and a wrong foot. Both feet are needed to move you forward. Try moving only on your right foot, and see how far you get. Similarly, in sailing this same principle applies—in beating upwind, it's necessary to tack to the left and right to move forward. Then why place so much emphasis on making only right decisions?

Lifecareering

Those who actively live *Life*-as-career are Lifecareerists. They know that *Life* is learning and that it includes everything. They realize that:

- they don't have to search for a career—they have one.
- they don't have to worry about losing it.
- they can trust their Career Compass—experience, intelligence, and intuition—to guide them forward and through changes.
- eventually, they'll know what they are to do.

- "life by the yard is hard; inch by
  inch it's a cinch."
- they don't have to fit other people's
  notions of who they are—or what
  they should be doing.
- they can find ways to support their needs.

Nature keeps itself in balance through cycles of death and birth. Lifecareerists also observe this principle: they know that, when one interest dies, another is born. *Life* keeps moving through cycles like the caterpillar en route to becoming a butterfly. Therefore, Lifecareerists don't *work* life, they *live* life.

By reading on, you'll learn more about what Lifecareering is and how to adopt this perspective in your own life. You'll also gain support for what you're doing and learn how to go about unfolding your purpose.

As you start to experience the concept of *Life-as-career,* you'll read about some ideas from the new science which will help to reinforce what you intuitively know. You won't even need a science background to understand these important principles since they're already in your experience. You'll also be exposed to some old ideas and assumptions that keep many people from fully living *Life*-as-career. Then I'll talk about looking for a work of your own. To do this, you'll want to know more about *fullering* which means doing work that gives you joy—not work that brings on a cardiac arrest or ulcers.

That's another subject we'll explore in these pages: how your attitudes and feelings affect your body. Hating your job adversely affects your physical health, including your blood pressure. You also will learn how natural decision making is to all life forms on earth—even to particles—so there's no need for instruction. This doesn't mean for you to ignore decision making entirely. All of us want to move for-

ward, but at our own rates. So, I'll discuss how to
advance your *Life*-as-career.

As you come to understand these concepts, you'll
know that your Career Compass—your experience,
your intelligence, and your intuition—is your most
valuable and reliable career guide, a gift from the universe. Seeing *Life*-as-career, you'll also realize that:

> You are led through your lifetime by your
> inner learning creature, the spiritual
> being that is your real self. You're always
> free to change your mind and choose a
> different future or a different past. Don't
> turn away from possible futures before
> you're certain you don't have anything
> more to learn from them (Bach, R. p. 63).

With this important new awareness, you'll be able
to create your own career philosophy. All you'll need
for this journey is your Career Compass.

Falling into Good Fortune

When you believe that *Life*-is-career, you begin
to place greater trust in *Life*. As you do, you find
yourself *attracting* good fortune.

That's the beauty of letting *Life work* for you.
Things evolve so easily. Temporary downturns also
become easier to accept because you realize that *Life*
is balanced. You may be in the valley now, but you've
nowhere to go but up. You simply trust *Life*. You
recognize that *Life* knows what it's doing—and
where it's going.

When you actively live *Life*-as-career, you tune
into your inner being. You hear your inner messages.
Then you align with them. We've all had the experience of knowing we need to do a certain thing only to
let our minds talk us out of it. Looking back, though,

we saw our intuition was right. When you follow your intuition, you do what feels right for you. That's attunement. When you act on that feeling, that's alignment. Then you experience *oneness*. You feel one with yourself and with *Life*. You feel whole.

This approach may seem simple, but it took many years of professional effort for the realization to mature in me. Even after it emerged full blown, I struggled with myself, my psyche. So, I surrendered to the power of these simple messages.

But, it still took courage and real mental effort to convince myself that the simple message *Life-is-career* could work in trying times. Like many, I viewed careers as something out there instead of coming from within myself. At last, I could let go and accept *Life* as the real career source.

When I focused on life and on my place in life, a pattern began to form. I discovered that what I need comes to me. Even what seemed like crises in my life invariably turned into opportunities. Sometimes, I was totally surprised. Lessons I needed to learn came to me. I found continual support while learning these lessons, and often they were painful. I saw a far greater design working than most professional or educational leaders might acknowledge. Some of them seemed downright puzzled when I tried to explain this simple process.

One reason this higher universal design works is that humans didn't invent it. Nor can humans (thank heavens) appoint a committee to change it. Every person on earth has access to this design. And this design seems to become more available to you when you focus on living *Life-as-career*. The more you tap into this force, the more it emerges to guide and direct you. It may seem contrary to our traditional views of *making things happen*. But, once you realize that it *works*, you'll happily modify your notion of making-things-happen and start relying more on your Career Compass.

   As you discover that this universal design works, you also become aware that the larger whole is essentially beautiful, although it may not seem so when you're experiencing its darker moments.

2

THE LIFECAREER SMORGASBORD

Differences
Traditional career emphasizes self-concept theory;
Lifecareer, the self conceiving.

One Soul Reflecting Upon the Process

Tune in for a moment on the reflections of Leigh
Wilson, as he ponders his *Life*-as-career:

> Caterpillars? They think small.
> All them green things know is: crawl.
> Butterflies, though, they think: high!
> Them guys are free, 'cause they know: fly!

Premises of my Life-as-career:

- Being a Gypsy is better than bolting fenders
  on Fords.
- If you've done it for more than a while,
  you've done it too long.

- Once you've learned it, get on with something new.
- If it doesn't feel good, get out.
- If it does feel good, you should probably still get out 'cause it probably won't for long.
- Life is like a smorgasbord. But, keep on moving down the table, or folks will jam up behind you.
- Don't stop at the pickled herring just because it's good.
- If you fall in love with somebody who feels about this like you do, you're the king of all you survey. If you don't, welcome to serfdom.
- If I had lived in 1849, I'd have been in the first wave up the hill to Sutter's Mill in the California gold rush.
- There's probably more of these, but you get the idea. Stability isn't my first priority.

Most of the above verities verify the inevitable.

Move on. Because:

- I get bored without a new challenge. I have a low boredom threshold.
- I need to be learning something new about the world, my profession, myself.
- I'm curious, but usually cautious, about what's around the next corner.
- I've never worked a job without having left more of myself than I got from The Company.

They've won every time.

- They gave me some money; I gave them my life. No company has ever really said, "Thank you, Leigh, for a piece of your life."

- Most people think I'm a transient of some sort. Can't keep a job. A bum. However, most people have put their heads where the sun don't shine, are being strangled by their own sphincters, and mistake that sensation for the feeling of success.

And so on. Oh, I:

- have an insatiable need to try new things. The reason is: why not?
- have had the most mobility of anybody in my industry (news media) that I know of anywhere. And am proud of it.
- have become disillusioned with the entire industry. Full of egos and showboats and empty suits.
- know as much about this industry as any living being. Only place to go would be into management in New York. Would rather wrestle crazed crocodiles in boiling oil in hell. This is to say, I've declined.
- enjoy people, recognize I'm sensitive about them and their problems. Have been around many troubled people (everyone in broadcasting), been through counseling myself, and find it challenging, intriguing. It feels good.

Therefore: Let's do it again, but this time, let's go for it:

Slam on the brakes, and change directions. Go to school, learn a new trade. See where it takes you (Wilson, 1986).

These words capture the beat of *Life*-in-career. But, let's move on down the smorgasbord of career and see what's there.

Career: The Gift That Keeps On Giving

Career Is a Gift

It came with your life. It calls for more active participation than any other gift you may receive. It also offers you greater rewards. Moreover, it's a gift that, once you realize it's yours, enables you to help others to realize it's *theirs,* as well. As you give the gift of this understanding to others, it grows within your own life. The more you give, the more you have to give.

If we all can pass along awareness of this gift to others, and let it continue to grow within us, humanity may one day reach a critical mass. That's the point at which enough of us recognize that *Life*-is-career—a gift—and that the power of this realization will explode and envelop the universe.

Life is a rough draft. Don't use too much energy trying to perfect it. It won't work.

Growth and Change

As you become aware that *Life*-is-career, you'll increasingly come to see the pattern and rightness of your actions—rightness for you. But be aware that this pattern may contain some continuing chaos. Without periodic disorganization and unrest, you'd feel stuck. Without change, and the uneasiness, pain, and confusion that often accompany it, you'd have no healthy shoots pushing through the old branches.

Growth and strength come from chaos and disorganization. This law seems to govern every life form in the universe. From a state of turmoil and disorder comes maintenance, growth, or the disappearance of the form. Atomic particles, for example, must find an electrical equilibrium, or they'll fly apart in a frenzy of spent energy. Similarly, planets find their equilibrium around suns, and moons find theirs around the planets.

Earth creatures also must survive ever-changing environmental threats. And galaxies composed of millions of suns must find a delicate balance of the universal forces or fall in upon themselves. Every form in the universe constantly seeks to escape chaos and to find harmony in its environment. Even you.

Consider the Caterpillar

When we think intelligence makes us superior to other life forms, consider how it also holds us back—or prevents us from moving forward. Consider the caterpillar. It goes along, chomping leaves contentedly. Then, suddenly, an unknown, irresistible change comes over it. Though the caterpillar may not understand this change, it simply accepts and prepares for it. Nature has equipped the caterpillar to meet this challenge. It's equipped us to do so as well—if we learn to let go and to stop resisting change.

Note how the caterpillar spins a cocoon to protect itself during the transformation to what it doesn't know. Then after a remarkable metamorphosis, it pushes out of the cocoon, dries its wings, and flies into the air, a surprised, free, and colorful butterfly.

Are we any less than the caterpillar? In meeting change have we the same measure of faith and acceptance? Think about it. Do you want to become a butterfly? Or do you use all your energies resisting change? Are you bent on staying a caterpillar merely because you're familiar with the role? Or because you fear change, like the caterpillar that spotted a butterfly and exclaimed, "You'll never get *me* up in one of those things!"

Opportunity Favors Everyone

Opportunity seems to favor the prepared. Yet, it also smiles on the unprepared as well. It's fine to prepare for your future, if that feels right to you. But if it doesn't, then do what feels right and what you know. *Life*-as-career can't be entirely free until you follow what you know. What comes along, comes along. You'll have to deal with it as part of your *Life*-as-career. And only you can do so. As Richard Bach suggests in his book *Illusions*: "Your only obligation in any lifetime is to be true to yourself."

Finding Your Own Footprints:
The Pooh Bear Approach

I spent many years heeding other people's notions of what career is. Then I decided to apply an approach I had read in *Winnie the Pooh*. In that popular book, the character Pooh Bear was doing what he called "tracking." He was walking around a spinnet bush and trying to determine who the paw tracks he saw on the ground in front of him belonged to. He thought they were Woozle and Wizzle tracks, because he was a bear of very small brain.

Recognizing when you're Pooh Bearing it — doing the same thing over and over — is one way to Lifecareer more fully.

So Pooh Bear continued walking around the spinnet bush, pursuing Woozles and Wizzles. After a while, he stopped. Then, carefully, he fit his own paw—perfectly—into one of the Woozle tracks. As he did, a very wonderful thing happened: he became wise to himself. Though Pooh was a bear of very small brain, he knew about getting wise to himself.

Catching On

Life Goes As Fast As It Goes

Pooh Bear knew that our life paths unfold from within. We can't unfold them any faster than they go. Simple as it sounds, it's true. Life unfolds at its own pace; we can't live it any faster. So why do we all keep trying too hard to do so? It only makes us angry and frustrated and out of sorts. Or, as another thoughtful creature, Pogo Possum, said, "We've met the enemy, and it is us."

If you follow your bliss, you put yourself on a kind of track that has been there all the while, waiting for you, and the life that you ought to be living is the one you are living. Wherever you are — if you are following your bliss, you are enjoying that refreshment, that life within you, all the time (p. 91).

Joseph Campbell - The Power of Myth

We've all had the experience of trying to rush through life, trying to get past difficult periods and put them *behind* us. But, that doesn't work. You don't need a Ph.D. to figure that out. You don't really need Pooh Bear or Pogo Possum to point it out. In getting from here to there in life, we sometimes go *left*. Learning from our *left* turns enables us to be our own best guide. But, if we don't learn from our *left* turns in life, like Pooh Bear, we'll keep retracing our steps along the same path. Then one day, we get smart and see that the footprints we continue to step in are our own.

Life-as-career is: moving forward; doing something right, then doing something left (often called wrong). We then correct, adjust, learn, improve, and move on again.

Working to Windward

Sailors understand this back and forth action. They call it *tacking*, or sailing against the wind. This means sailing close to the wind (beating) in a zigzag direction to reach a destination directly in front of you. In this way, you can sail into a headwind and fulfill your intention, if you're willing to exert some effort.

Similarly, *life-tacking* will take you where you want to go. But, even if your intention is in sight, you probably won't be able to sail directly to it and grab it. The ever-changing winds of life usually prevent this. So you have to tack first one way, then the other, constantly beating into the headwind. Each tack in itself is a partial *error*, a failure to directly reach your destination. It takes real effort and time, but it works. You're making the very wind that seems to be keeping you from your intention *work* for you. And with patience, skill, and determination, you move ahead even closer to your chosen port.

Here to there, then, is a series of errors. Buckminster Fuller, in his cosmic fairy tale, *Tetrascroll: Goldilocks and the Three Bears*, tells how Goldilocks drew a sketch of Mommy Bear in reverse. Then she realized that if it was to be printed directly from her drawing, it would require an original mirror-image master. But Goldilocks decided to leave her sketch that way to remind everyone that: "We can only get from there to here by a series of errors; forward to the right, then a correcting movement to the left, and so on; each time reducing error but never eliminating it" (Page xxi).

As you start to live *Life*-as-career, it's important

to learn to love and respect all your decisions—the left and the right ones. All of them serve to make you what you are. The sooner you realize there are no wrong turns in life, the more peaceful you can feel about yourself and your decisions. They're simply turns. And how others may view them are only judgments.

When we begin to realize that our *errors* are merely *left* turns, we start to move closer to the truth. We gain a whole new feeling about ourselves and our experiences. Isn't it wonderful to find out how much life is teaching us, instead of thinking about how much we've failed?

The Wallenda Factor:
Energy Directed at Falling or Failing

The *Lifecareer* process encourages putting all your energies into succeeding—on your own terms. This is important, according to the findings of a nationwide study of leadership qualities done by Professor Warren Bennis. One of these findings, cited by Bennis in the book *Leaders: Strategies for Taking Charge,* is what he calls the "Wallenda Factor," after famed tightrope-walker Karl Wallenda. "The only time I feel really alive," Wallenda once told his family, "is when I'm walking the tightrope."

In 1973, at age 71, during a tightrope-walk in San Juan, Puerto Rico, Karl Wallenda plunged to his death. He fell, his wife later speculated, because, before that walk, for the first time in his life, Karl Wallenda had thought about falling. He seemed to refocus all his energies, she said, onto falling and failing.

According to Bennis, when embarking on a new relationship or other venture, it's important to focus your energies on making it work—and not on the fear of failure.

If you start putting your energies into falling, into failing, into wallowing in the

mistakes you might make (which isn't to
say you don't look at the down-side risks),
then you're more likely to fail. The Wallenda Factor is crucial in leadership. But, in
a way, I'm talking as much about life as I
am about leadership. Because when I'm
talking to my daughter, who's starting a
career in acting, where the hazards of not
making it are very real, or where you're
talking about writing a book, I think you
have to walk the tightrope. You have to put
your energies into making it (Bennis, 1983).

Recognize Yourself
by Your Descriptions

An important *Lifecareer* skill is identifying your
own issues. "How can I do that?" By listening to what
you say about others. You've probably heard it said
that something we don't like in another person—a
trait, a habit, a way of walking or talking—is probably something we don't like in ourselves as well. But
what we don't realize is that the reverse also may be
true: what we like in someone else is probably what
we like in ourselves.

Another widespread belief is that what you don't
like in someone else is what you *fear* becoming. And
most valid of all is Ilya Prigogine's statement, "Nature is part of us as we are part of it. We can recognize ourselves in the description we give to it." In
other words, anything we say about another person
is largely a reflection of our own inner issues and
problems. It says little about the person we comment
about. And it says a lot about *us*.

A client of mine who recently came to realize this
says she doesn't have nearly as much to say now
about others. She knows that her comments reflect
her own inner issues, and unless she's willing to take
responsibility for these issues she doesn't comment.

This has distanced her from many of her friends and co-workers. Why? Because she no longer joins them in criticizing other people—what they wear, how they act, what they think. She's found that her new awareness doesn't make her popular with the group. She's also found that the group members enjoy and seem to gain more cohesion from collectively agreeing on the inferior traits of other people.

According to noted physicist David Bohm, in *On Freedom and the Individual:*

> As one perceives the inferiority of the other person, implying one's own 'superiority,' one experiences a short, sharp burst of intense pleasure. To sustain the pleasure, the mind continues with further false thoughts along this line while hiding from itself the fact that it is doing so (p. 22).

The intense pleasure and later *high* one gains through self-deception may be as addictive as the post-performance *high* experienced by some athletes, who continually try to recapture it. So those who experience intense pleasure and gain group cohesion by not acknowledging their own issues may find it more difficult to become self aware. *Lifecareer* is about recognizing and taking responsibility for our individual issues.

Taking Charge

Free Will, Choice, or Destiny?

What happens to us depends largely on our choices. Each day, we make our future and then watch it come true. Some people call this *taking charge* of our lives. Others believe in *destiny*. Regarding this question of free will versus destiny, Dr. Fred Alan Wolf, in his book, *Taking the Quantum*

Leap: The New Physics for Non-Scientists, suggests that "Both views are wrong and right at the same time. We are the creators of our reality and the victims of our creation."

Here's how that works. Choose one of the following letters:

A   B   C

(See Page 258)   (See Page 259)   (See Page 261)

Turn, now, to the page indicated under the letter you picked and you'll find that I knew which one you'd choose. You were free to choose among the above letters. However, once chosen, you became linked to the destiny of that letter. So, we create our reality and are receivers of our creations.

In work-career terms, consider Grant, who lives in New York City. When Grant suddenly lost his job, he realized he had three choices: (1) he could sit around feeling depressed; (2) he could go out and try to get a job; or (3) he could create his own work. Having only a few dollars left to live on, he didn't want to spend time going from interview to interview. So he decided to create his own work. But what could he do? Then it dawned on him—why not clean the windshields of cars stalled in traffic? He was bound to pick up a few dollars in tips. So he got a small box, put some glass cleaner and rags in it, and walked out onto the city streets. Spotting a traffic jam ahead, he began to clean the windshields of the cars waiting in line. Most of the drivers seemed pleased. Some gave him tips. Soon, he was taking in about $600 a week.

Grant chose his reality. His options were to feel self-employed rather than depressed. And it worked for him. It worked so well you might even say it was meant to be. On hearing of Grant's success, several other people decided to try cleaning windshields, too,

but few were as successful as he. Maybe it just wasn't
in the cards for them. Several years later, the Mayor
of New York was trying to prevent this kind of activity as some of the cleaners demanded the amount
they wanted for the job and were no longer accepting tips.

Not everyone responds to the loss of a job by
allowing life to unfold a positive new direction, as
Grant did. Consider Tony, for example. After nearly
30 years on the job, he was terminated. Despite his
efforts, he couldn't find work. Then the savings-and-
loan association foreclosed on his home. Tony went
back to his former hometown to look for work, but
found nothing. After many months of job hunting
without success, he decided to take matters into his
own hands. One Friday morning, Tony and his wife,
Kay, left their dog with a friend. They drove around
until their car ran out of gasoline. Then Tony got out
of the car, opened the trunk, and took out a rifle. He
shot his wife, then himself. Free will or destiny? Both.
We create our reality, thereby fulfilling our destiny. A
self-chosen one. Yet, each of our lives is interwoven
with very intricate, delicate threads that influence the
choices we make in one way or another.

At 32, for example, author Buckminster Fuller,
inventor of the geodesic dome, also considered sui-
cide. However, he then decided against it. Instead,
Fuller made a commitment to his life. He determined
to find out what one person could do without "capital
or any kind of wealth, cash savings, account monies,
credit, or university degree." Fuller wanted to learn
what he could do that even corporations or whole
nations could not do to improve the quality of human
life on earth. To these ends, Fuller committed himself
to doing:

> ...my own thinking, confining it to only
> experientially gained information, and
> with the products of my own thinking

and intuition, to articulate my own innate
motivational integrity, instead of trying to
accommodate everyone else's opinions,
credos, educational theories, romances,
and mores, as I had in my earlier life
(Fuller, 1981a, p. 125).

Free will versus destiny? Both. Yet, when we
meet tragedy, it's difficult, as Gregory Bateson,
author of *Mind and Nature: A Missing Unity,* suggests, to understand that, "whatever the ups and
downs of detail within our limited experience, the
larger whole is primarily beautiful" (p. 19).

3

YOUR LIFECAREER JOURNEY

Differences
Traditional career suggests control of life; Lifecareer supports cooperation with life.

Let's journey through life and see if you can recognize some of your own experiences. They'll help you to see how society programs us as we grow up.

In the Crib

You're an infant. Alone at night, you wake, stare into the darkness, and cry. Your mother and father don't hear your frightened little sounds. You feel lost and helpless. You are afraid to be alone without your parents. You don't yet understand what life is all about. What is your career at this early stage? It is simply your life. Chances are that, even before you left the hospital, you began to receive secondary career messages. Recent research findings indicate that nurses, when showing babies to visiting family members, tend to hold infant girls close and protectively. Infant boys, however, are held at arm's length and bounced.

In the Playpen

Success! You finally pull yourself up for the first time. You're standing on your own two feet. Oh, no—thump! You fall. You learn that air won't support you. Neither will your parents, now that they've seen you stand. But you haven't yet caught on to the need for keeping your balance and for moving forward first on one foot, then on the other. Adults already know that you can't walk on your right foot alone, that it takes both the right foot and the left foot for balance. Yet, as you grow older, they will start to tell you about *right* or *wise* decisions. Ignored are the important *left* decisions that balance your life and teach you. In the playpen, though, you don't worry about it. You're too busy careering around in your special space.

At School

As your Lifecareer progresses, you have to make decisions about learning to read, write, do math, and communicate. You have to decide what classes to take. And though you haven't yet caught on how to do it, you try to decide what you want to be. People in your life push you this way and that way. They tell you what you *should* do. They make suggestions and impose their views and perceptions (life fiction) on you. Yet the new physics shows that none of us can know reality—we merely have ideas about it. For example, scientists have found that the smallest elementary particles can exist either as matter or as energy, but not as both at the same time. Their existence as matter or energy depends on how the individual physicist chooses to *view* them.

Therefore, we all create our own realities. We

make them up as we go along. So it's important to
recognize that how you see the world is *your* reality—no one else's. You are learning to listen to that
voice inside you that whispers what's best for you.
It's the voice of your inner guide. It's your Career
Compass spinning the millions of pieces of information around and periodically giving you readings. It
knows what's good for you—even when you're uncertain.

---

*Don't let anyone save you from your
experience, it's all you have.*

Where is your career at this confusing time?
Simply, in life.

You're in the ninth grade. You're getting used to
new classes, new teachers, new friends (*big* kids)
from a wider social circle. Your sex hormones are on
the move. You haven't caught on yet to what's happening, but you've been in love three times this
month. You may also have a new girlfriend or boy-
friend you don't understand. And you care what
your friends think about you. Are you doing the *right*
things to gain their approval? To complicate your
life, your parents are getting a divorce. You feel angry, guilty, and somehow responsible for that.

When you entered the ninth grade, you may
have attended a Welcoming Assembly the second
day of school. There the principal's message went
something like:

> Welcome back, boys and girls. We hope
> you had a great summer. The staff has
> worked hard to provide you with inter-
> esting and challenging courses. These
> courses will help you to decide what
> you want to do with your life. You must

decide this week and sign up by next
Monday. Remember there will be no
schedule changes after classes start—
so choose carefully.

On top of this, your school counselor tells you, "If
you don't take the *right* classes, you may not get ac-
cepted into the college you want."
College? You look at her in disbelief.
But before you can pursue it, she's pressing you,
"Now, what do you want to do when you graduate
from college?"
Your face goes blank. Graduation from college is
years away. And full-time work? Centuries away.
You can't imagine relating ninth-grade social studies
or wood shop to any kind of life work.
Where is your career now? Simply in life.

At College

They said you should go to college. Now that
you are, *they* tell you that you must decide what you
want to do in life. This is it. You must select your
classes accordingly. You must concentrate on what
you will pursue as a long-term, single-income occupation. Amidst all the activity, you can barely hear
your own voice. What's your career now? Life.
Well, you've made it through the first year of
college with a safe assortment of basic *liberal arts*
courses. You noticed they were neither liberal nor art,
but who can question academe? And now you're a
sophomore. Your advisement officer tells you it's
time to declare a major. What's a major? You're uncertain, because you lack information. You still have
little idea what to *do* when you graduate. Yet, here
you are, sitting in an Advisement Office in the second
year of your college. After all, college is expensive
enough (your parents point out) even if you do know
what you want to *be*. If you don't, there are cheaper

ways to find out. But here you are—in college.

Your adviser waits impatiently for you to declare your major, so he or she can move you out and move the next student in. You feel that tight, shallow breathing in your chest. A cold, prickly feeling starts inside. Your hands grow clammy. "It seems as if everyone else but me knows what they want to do. What's *wrong* with me?" Then you hear someone say, "Quick, declare something!"

Reading your own Career Compass, not someone else's, can cause you to follow the road less traveled, which can make all the difference.

Where is your career now? It's where it has always been, in life. "But how do I explain that to my adviser," you ask, "who keeps thrusting 'shoulds' on me and asking me to *choose* a career? How can I tell him that *life* is my career?"

After College

Now, you're a college graduate. You declared and majored in geology, but you don't know how you will earn money. You feel no burning desire to climb the Himalayas, unearthing rare stones. You don't want to search for oil in Saudi Arabia. Still, you majored in geology, and you don't know much about anything else. You've been behind the ivy-covered walls for four years.

Where is your career now? Where it has always been—in life.

Out in the World

You're armed with a high school diploma or a

college degree, or both. But you're still unsure. As you pursue your identity, you still haven't caught on to the importance of listening to your inner voice. But you will—with time and maturity. As you live, your needs, your strengths, your choices, your courage, your ability to act—all will become clearer.

If you are in the line of someone else's self interest, you win. If not, you still win, but not in the way you expected. Instead, you win a learning.

Your World Shifts

You lose your job. Do you also lose your career? Not unless you think you do.

You're an adult. You think society expects stability in your work career. It expects you to be productive and to contribute your share to society, which, after all, enabled you to get where you are. At least, that's what you've been led to believe. Society also expects you to support your family in the proper manner in the proper home, as Ozzie and Harriet did in the 1960s TV sitcom of the same name (although Ozzie didn't appear to have an occupation). You think your work career should be established.

What you may not realize is that most American families don't follow a smooth upward *should* curve on the chart of life. If you graphed the average American Lifecareer, a saw-tooth line would probably cover the chart. Imagine yourself into each of these all-too-real contemporary roles:

You're on Welfare

You don't have a job, and there isn't one in sight. It's hard for you to believe you have a career. What is it? What could your career possibly be when you find yourself in the lowest level of the socioeconomic scale. There are so many things you have not had the opportunity to see and do. You, therefore, are limited by your lack of experience and cultural advantage.

Nonetheless, life is your career, job or no job, possibilities or no possibilities.

You're a Graduate Student

You've earned a master's degree. You're working on your Ph.D. (*They* told you that you would need one to teach.) Now you're worried that there won't be a place for you when you get it. People say there aren't many teaching jobs available, particularly in your specialty. You don't know what to do with your Ph.D.—or with your life, for that matter. In what work career could you best put your education and experience to work? You need direction.

Where is your career? In what you're doing now.

You're a Factory Worker

For 24 years, you worked in the General Electric flat-iron plant in Ontario, California. The plant has been shut down. General Electric has relocated it to Singapore. This is the only work you know—you have worked in that plant since you were 18. You're angry and depressed. You can't understand why a foreign worker should have your job. You don't know what to do. You worry constantly. You have no direction. But you *do* have a family to support. While your spouse works, both paychecks are barely enough to support the five of you. You need work direction quickly, along with income.

Where is your career, anyway? In life, of course.

You're a Displaced Worker

You had worked for 16 years in a large corporation, fighting your way up the management ladder. Then a conglomerate took over your company, and you suddenly found yourself under a new administrator. Your philosophies didn't coincide. Now you're trying to make it on your own, as a consultant. But it's scary out there. You don't have the resources of a large company behind you. There seems to be no model for you in this new work. You're on a strange path, and the trail is not marked. You find yourself pioneering a whole new way.

So you follow your Career Compass—your experience, intelligence, and intuition. While it feels pretty good at times, it can also be frightening. Can you keep your perspective as your inner voice guides you? You can if you *let* it. You're following your own cues even though you're walking through a strange land. And, after all, you can't do it any other way.

You're a Homemaker

Your husband was fired from an executive job. Cutbacks, they called it. He feels he has no career now. He gets dressed every morning, just as though he's going to work. Only he goes downstairs instead and works at his desk. His present occupation is reading help-wanted ads and calling companies to check on job openings. He's frustrated. You're frustrated. You don't know how to help him. You encourage him. You tell him, "It's all right." But you wonder if the nice *work and homemaker careers* the two of you have built will survive.

Where is your career? In your life—though it may seem rough at the moment. Think about what the two of you know, what you can do. And put it into action.

You're a Working Single Parent

You have a master's degree in theater arts. You

teach part-time and earn $2,000 a semester. You've also started to write and submit free lance articles to entertainment magazines, but you haven't sold any yet. So you do part-time work to help support yourself and your two children. Your closest friend, who has the same degree as you, is in her fourth year at a large corporation. When you learn that she earns $60,000 a year, you are stunned—and deflated. "What did I do wrong?" you ask.

You wonder if you're going in the right direction, following the right work career. Then you stop and know that you are following what is right for you because it's fulfilling. It nourishes your soul, and the voice within you tells you that, for you, money is not the primary measure of success. You believe it. You know it. You also know that *Life*-is-career, even though money is widely touted as the report card of success.

You're a Secure Job Fossil

You have taught school for 20 years. It's the first day of a new semester. You suddenly have the unsettling feeling you have been teaching this course and looking out at this sea of faces for several centuries. You realize that you are tired of teaching. You are ready to do something different and interesting. And you don't have the haziest notion what that might be.

Where is your career? In life, and in what you choose to do with it.

You're a Returning Homemaker

You have raised three children. Now they are grown and gone. You have never worked outside of the home, but now you would like to. The idea of having a job intrigues you. Only you feel you have no marketable skills. You don't know how or where you would fit in. So you sit at home, bored, frustrated, feeling a little sorry for yourself.

Where is your career? In life, of course. If you have successfully nurtured and raised a family, you have years of solid experience that probably can be put to good use out there.

You're about to Retire

You are 65. You've spent the past 40 years working for The Company. This is your final week on the job. The party's Friday night. You gave The Company the lion's share of your life. You gave it your energy, and your care, and your attention—frequently at the expense of your family, your friends, yourself. As you look back, it suddenly feels as if the river of life is sweeping you toward the rapids. There is no avoiding them. Their roar fills your ears. Your life-craft has been drifting along calmly all these years. Suddenly, it seems to crash and spin out of control. Memories flash across your mind: pictures of things you had meant to do, jobs you had intended to try, occupations you wanted to retrain for, work you could have done—but didn't.

Instead you chose to remain in the calm, safe waters. And now it's too late. Or is it?

Where is your career now? It's in the rest of your life—and in what you choose to do with it.

You're Retired

You have been retired for nearly a year. You've repaired everything in the house and the car, as well. Now time is starting to hang heavy on your hands. You follow your wife around like a puppy. She shoos you away. So you sit, staring out the window. Is this what I worked so hard for all of those years? You know you'll wake up tomorrow morning wondering what to do.

You thought you would have some direction

after retirement. But where is it? And where is your career? In life, of course.

What We All Have in Common

Common Traits

Let's look at the common threads apparent in the lives of the people just cited.

First, most of them believe their careers are somewhere outside of them, separate from themselves. They do not realize that life and career are one. Career is not merely that part of your life you devote to a job, work, occupation, or profession. How you choose to earn your living *is* only a part of your *Life*-as-career. The information you gain as you live every second unfolds into what becomes your career path.

Second, many of the people just cited seem to think that others know more than they do about how to get from A to B, from this job to that job, from apprenticeship to success. In fact, most people believe that other people—the omnipresent *they*—all know what they're doing with their lives. Those who believe this also may see themselves as part of a terribly oppressed minority who cannot get their lives together. If this describes you, step back and take a harder look at others. You may be surprised to find they are in deeper alligator-water than you are!

Common Needs

We all have need for food, shelter, safety, love, and feelings of belonging, self-esteem, and personal growth. According to psychologist Abraham Maslow, however, our survival needs must be met before we can attend to creativity and growth.

For a number of people throughout the United States, these basic survival needs are not being met.

An estimated 29 million have incomes below the
poverty level. About 5.5 million are unemployed. Another 6 million unemployed who want to work have
given up looking. Over 3 million people are homeless—without shelter. Many sleep in alleys, on streets,
or park benches, and in subways, bus terminals, or in
packing boxes, and other makeshift shelters.

Pulling the Work-Career Plow

Many of those who have survival needs met still
plod through life like a bullock pulling a plow, doing
what others think should be done. They not only pull
the education plow, but the work-career plow and
the family plow.

What keeps the harness on? Being told, almost
from infancy, about *right* attitudes, *right* beliefs.
Mores, sociologists call them. (But remember that is
their fiction—all made up from their reality.) Tradi-
tions. Here's how it goes: if you really want to *get*
somewhere in life, you have to dress *right*, talk *right*,
have the *right* attitudes, play it *right*, know how to
use power *right*, and build the *right* career by know—
ing and playing by the *right* rules. That is what
passes for the road to success. What we're not told is
that the most important success *is living life on our
own terms.* This is the kind of success everyone of us
can achieve.

You and Society and Your Lifecareer

In all of the life situations I've described in this
chapter, the common thread that runs among them is
Life-is-career. Every thread of experience you draw
through the fabric of your life adds to its texture. If
you can see each thing you do as a single thread of
life—if you can see the pattern of your life-fabric
forming as a result of them—then you can be the
weaver of your life.

4

THE NEW SCIENCE AND LIFECAREER

Differences

Traditional career suggests that the parts *equal* the whole.
Lifecareer acknowledges that the whole
organizes the parts.

The Way We Were

It used to be thought that the physical laws, such as those that govern time and the tides, were fixed. The universe was believed to run with predictable, clock-like precision. So were our lives. Thus, if our lives, our careers, didn't operate with clock-like precision, the solution was simple: find what was wrong and fix it. If our health failed, the solution was simple. Find the problem part and fix it.

René Descartes and Sir Isaac Newton, two eminent scientists of the 17th century, devised the theories that were to govern broad areas of scientific thought for more than 300 years. Descartes, for example, held that scientific knowledge should be certain. He felt we should believe only those things which can be fully known and substantiated, beyond all doubt. He also regarded nature as a perfect machine and the mind as a separate entity from the body. In a similar vein, Newton saw the universe as a great clock. Take it apart and study its inner workings, he said, and you'll understand the universe. This notion worked very well when applied to the movement of planets, manned space flights, and modern technology. But, when Newton's theory was applied to the atomic and sub-atomic worlds, it fell short. "Scientists became painfully aware that the basic concepts, their language, and their whole way of thinking (analyses) were inadequate to deal with these new atomic phenomena" (Capra, 1983). They suffered a crisis of perception. The way they were used to thinking about the universe no longer worked completely.

As Don Bradley, a sports writer notes, life is like a rickety card table. Bradley suggests that when we're born, that old-fashioned cardboard table with rickety folding legs is set up in front of us, then God dumps a huge jigsaw puzzle on it and says: "When you're finished you'll understand why you're here." Most people finish the puzzle when they are in middle age. Often they spend the remainder of their lives protecting the puzzle.

This is also true of scientists. In earlier eras, scientists carefully pieced together their Newtonian jigsaw puzzle, then hovered over it protectively. But, when Einstein and other new physicists emerged, kicking the card table, the Newtonian puzzle of the universe scattered on the floor. This doesn't mean Newton was wrong. It simply means that his view of the universe was limited; it may not work like a clock after all.

Just as social scientists created their reality with

an eye to Newton's theory, they also looked with interest at the new physics theory of the universe. Presto! New Age social thinkers embraced this new theory and took off in a different direction. Now they could stop trying to mold themselves into what others thought they should be. They could see and acknowledge at last that they were whole and could stop trying to repair the parts that weren't broken in the first place. Many scientists of all kinds now were seeing the whole rather than the parts. They saw with fascination how each aspect fit in with all the others.

We are not victims of the world we see, we are victims of how we see the world.

Author unknown

Noted physicist, David Bohm, in his book *Wholeness and the Implicate Order,* advanced the idea that the whole organizes the parts, not the reverse, which contributed to an emerging new perspective. New Age career counselors began to follow the lead. Suddenly, the old story of three blind men describing an elephant took on new meaning. One felt the elephant's trunk and said an elephant is thin, like a snake. Another felt its leg and said an elephant is round, like a post. The third felt its side and said an elephant is flat, like a house. All were correct, but none was describing the whole creature. By considering only its parts, they were misled.

The new physics scientists then gave social scientists a further bonus. On studying tiny sub-atomic particles, they discovered that the observer's perspective determined the qualities of the particle studied. If the scientist was looking for mass, the particle had mass. If the scientist was looking for energy, the same particle had energy. From this, social scientists began to recognize that we create our own reality.

The mass/energy duality introduced two other important new physics principles: *complementarity* and *uncertainty*. The principle of complementarity, which is akin to our notion of *opposites,* explains why both mass and energy *cannot* be observed at the same time in the same particle. Something can't be both black and white at the same time. But the new physics approaches this duality in another way. A particle actually may have *both* mass and energy. However, when you try to measure either, you can only look for one at a time. Therefore, you can only see *either* mass *or* energy. This brings up the principle of uncertainty. By focusing on measuring the mass of the particle, energy in that same particle can't be observed. And since we regard reality as what is observable, we say that it doesn't exist.

One of the problems with the principles of complementarity and uncertainty is that you can never dissect one from the other, as Newton would have proposed. This brings up a third principle that is ever present in the new physics: *connectedness.* Simply stated this means that the universe cannot be divided indefinitely and still be the same. The universe is made up of relationships. For example, the centuries-old process of *bleeding* a patient to rid him or her of *bad blood* often resulted in death, because blood and life are highly connected. So are the relationships within the universe.

Each of us has in some way found that the universe cannot be separated into independent parts. It can be understood only by looking at the whole and recognizing the intricate web of relationships that comprise it. The universe, our bodies, and the very earth beneath our feet are far more complex than we may realize. Each part is both more individual and more random than once thought. And each part is more connected to every other part than many realize. Thus, if things are not working out as you think they should, in a neat, orderly progression, it needn't mean that any of your parts are faulty. It just means that is the way life works and you are part of life.

Consider how many different, individual parts compose your body, your mind and brain, your thought and spirit. Can you separate these different parts from one another and still have *you*? Of course not! Said Admiral James Stockdale, USN, of his confinement as a prisoner of war in Vietnam, "Our minds had a tremendous capacity for invention and introspection, but had the weakness of being...part of our bodies." He remembered how Descartes had separated mind and body. Stockdale's response, "Gosh, how I wish Descartes could have been right, but he's wrong."

To illustrate the connectedness of your mind to your body, try curling your index finger. Consider how your thoughts, brain waves, and nerve signals prompted your muscle fibers to act as you asked them to. You cannot understand the complex functions involved in curling your finger by studying only your finger. You must study your whole being and all of its inter-workings.

Now apply this same approach to a center fielder chasing a long fly ball. Consider the billions of complementary signals coursing back and forth between his brain, his nerves, and his muscles as he pursues the play. He races at top speed. He judges the trajectory of the ball. He directs his glove to exactly the right place in space at the right moment. He signals his body to leap into the air, his hand thrust upward. Then he protects himself as he falls, the ball clutched safely in his glove.

The ultimate failure of the Newtonian theory shows that it isn't the golden path, only a special-case theory. Though many applied this theory to people, their lives, and our interest here, their *Life*-as-career, it became clear to some in the social sciences and to increasing numbers of others that Newton's clockwork approach wasn't working. The great break came in the 1920s with the emergence of the so-called new physics. Sixty years later, we find ourselves just beginning to understand what it means to us personally and to our culture.

What does the new physics do that earlier scientific theories didn't do? It confirms what we've all always known down deep—that the universe is complementary, uncertain, and connected. Each of these principles, in turn, supports the *Life*-as-career idea.

Life is programmed for success.

A recurring theme in this book is that *compelling parallels exist between the reality of the microscopic physical world and the social level of our everyday human experience.* We're merely larger, more complex composites of the atomically small. From particles to humans, we're each a part of the *life* process. And the *Lifecareer* perspective works best for us when we recognize that we are part of nature and nature is part of us.

But Let's Not Make This a Physics Lesson

"But, I've never studied physics," you may be saying, "and certainly not new physics. I don't even know much about science."

The good news is that you don't have to formally study new physics to understand what I'm saying about its relationship to career development. You already understand it. You *live* it. The new physics principles more accurately describe how life works. And you're a living example of life. You're programmed for success. Sure, you kick your card table occasionally—or someone else does—and then you have trouble seeing the whole picture. But the universe continues to make order out of randomness, which often looks like chaos. And a good part of our life work is making order. We all do that daily and continually. We do it naturally.

"What does all of this have to do with my *Lifecareer?*" you ask.

Plenty. Just read on as I share with you what I've learned—and gained—by using the new physics principles as a daily *attitude* about life. You'll also read about new physics at work in the lives of others. As you come to understand these principles, you'll realize you've always known them. The question is will you acknowledge that you know them?

Some Cosmic Lifecareer Principles

Let's return to the new physics principles we examined earlier and see how they affect your views of life—for the better.

Complementarity

Noted physicist, Niels Bohr, introduced the principle of complementarity. Fritjof Capra, in his book *The Turning Point,* notes that Bohr considered "...the particle picture and the wave picture two complementary descriptions of the same reality. Both pictures are needed to give a full account of the atomic reality but both are to be applied within limitations set by the uncertainty principle" (Page 79). Simply stated, the universe is complementary. Like the Chinese yin/yang, opposites relate in a complementary way. However, complementarity introduces uncertainty because when you focus on one part, you miss the others.

Here's a diagram that helps to illustrate this point. Stare directly at, and *only* at, the bull's-eye (Life) in the center:

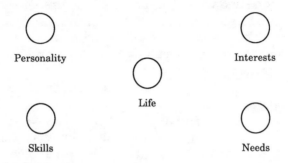

Note how the outer circles no longer seem as clear when you focus on the center. You are aware that the outer circles exist, but the construction of your eyes allows you to *see* only a very small area sharply. The reason for this is that only a very small group of highly sensitive cells, at the back of the eyeball, *see* sharply. How we see life is very similar to how we see the components in this diagram. Our physical and mental make-up enables most of us to see—or think about—only one thing at a time.

Hence, we tend to focus on the central issues in our lives, and overlook or don't see many of the other issues on the outskirts of our awareness. Added to this, we don't always see what we think we do. Much of what we see is the product of our illusions. Other valuable information is sidelined because we don't trust what we're seeing—and what it may say about us.

Robert Ornstein in his book, *The Psychology of Consciousness,* has an interesting proposition. He shows A, B, and C written horizontally (across), and 12, 13, and 14 written vertically (up and down).

Stop now and in your book margin or on a separate piece of paper write A, B, and C across and above the B write 12 and below the B write 14. Write the "B" as you see it written here. Now look at it.

When you read from top to bottom, the center character looks like a "13," because you expect to see a number. When you read from left to right, it looks like the letter "B," because you anticipate seeing a letter. Though both views are correct, they are totally different. You can focus on only one thing at a time, and this introduces *uncertainty*.

Complementarity in Lifecareer

When you recognize that neither a wave nor a particle alone completely describes the universe—it takes both to do so—then you realize that the same is true for you. It takes personality, interests, needs, courage, confidence—and much more—to fully describe you. Yet, when you focus on only one of these factors, you miss seeing the others.

Similarly, when you look for opportunity in one direction, you miss seeing it in other directions. We have all been told, "If you don't focus, you won't make the grade." But not focusing and casting around for information from various places is what gives us what we *need* to eventually focus.

A gifted student recently dropped out of college because: (1) he felt he was too young to narrow down his options; and (2) he felt he hadn't experienced enough to decide on a major. This young man realized he was focusing on math and science because these had been his primary subjects. He knew that, in doing so, he was missing other possibilities. This illustrates the *complementarity* principle of the new physics. When the young man dropped out of college to explore these other possibilities, he experienced some uncertainty about doing so, but he also trusted life. This uncertainty is another principle of the new physics. The young man was a student of the new physics. He not only believed the mathematics of it, he believed its power in his experience.

Consider how the complementarity principle re-
lates to being unemployed. When we focus on one
possibility, we miss out on others. But our relatives
and friends usually urge us to focus on a given job
area and go for it. It's difficult to focus before we
know what's possible. Yet, staying loose, looking
around, can give us the feeling of being without direction. That's uncomfortable and makes it even
harder for us to continue to check out possibilities.
We also worry that we should be doing something
more. Finding possibilities, though, is a matter of information gathering. Then it may be time to focus.
But only *you* know when that time has come.

---

*If the history of humanity or modern
science has any lasting certainty to offer
us, it is...that it is entirely possible for
rational individuals to be absolutely
certain about notions which later prove
to be utterly preposterous.*

Deane Juhan - Job's Body

The Uncertainty Principle

The Heisenberg Uncertainty Principle suggests
that, when you focus on one aspect of something,
you miss other aspects and meanings, introducing
uncertainty. This happens because you're dealing
with interrelated pairs of concepts which can't be
defined at the same time in a precise way. You'll recall the college student cited earlier who felt he
hadn't experienced enough in life to select a college
major. So he dropped out of school and began to explore life. However, the other side of the problem is

that dropping out of college increased his stress level. His family felt good about his future, but his friends worried about it. They asked him, "How can you possibly make it if you don't finish college?" Added to this was the stress of moving, changing what he did with his time, and changing his social group—all of which caused tremendous uncertainty and fear.

When you look at an object through a microscope, you see more individual parts. However, without a microscope, the whole can be seen. We are always moving around the parts within the whole. We are always experiencing uncertainty.

Here's another illustration of complementarity and uncertainty. Two cars have collided in an intersection. A police officer is interviewing three witnesses to the accident:

Police Officer:	What happened?
Person A:	The car ran a red light.
Person B:	No, the light was green.
Person C:	I didn't see the color of the light.

What you see depends on where you're focused and what you're looking for. Taking this a step further, Douglas Hofstadter, in his book *Gödel, Escher, and Bach: An Eternal Golden Braid,* discusses Gödel's theorem, which holds that no set of mathematical axioms exists which is without unspecified terms. In short, no perfect explanatory system exists. It's merely one of our illusions. Perfection is an ideal—not an experience.

Uncertainty and Your Work Career

Now translate *uncertainty* into *work career.* There's no way to prepare for a work career that will *guarantee* you anything. Why? Because only in an absolutely stable, clock-like environment is a reasonably accurate prediction possible, and such an environment *doesn't exist.* We live in an ever-changing society and in an unstable world. No one knows what's ahead.

James O'Toole of the Center for Futures Study at the University of Southern California observes:

> We simply don't know what specific knowledge people will need after their school years, because what people need to know is changing moment by moment. The best education for the future will be one that *develops the general ability to think clearly and use information well* (emphasis added, 1982a).

From a Machine to a Dynamic Whole

Today, the universe is viewed by scientists not as a machine made up of independent parts, but as an organic, ecological, interrelated whole—an intricate web of relationships. Or as 19th Century naturalist John Muir observed, "When we try to pick out anything by itself, we find it hitched to everything else in the universe."

Everything, then, is connected with everything else—even work and death, though not always in ways you might think. For example, pioneering research done by M. Harvey Brenner, medical sociologist at Johns Hopkins University, into long-term economic fluctuations and corresponding health trends, found that unemployment can be hazardous to your well being. The study linked the 14 percent increase in unemployment in the United States between 1973-74 with the following: an overall increase of 46,000 deaths of which 29,000 were attributed to heart disease. And, 8,400 more people were hospitalized for mental conditions, 577,000 more arrested, and 403 more homicides happened. Further, the increase in annual changes in business failure rate was associated with an increase of 95,000 cardiovascular deaths. The link between unemployment, business failures, and social havoc is clear.

Language Matters

Norman Cousins, author of *Anatomy of an Illness* recalls meeting with hundreds of cancer patients. What struck him most sharply was how much these patients' conditions worsened when they learned they had cancer. The simple knowledge that they were victims of a dread disease made them lose hope—and somehow shut down their bodies' own immune systems. As their brain signals triggered these physiological responses, they became less able to fight the disease.

Cousins also tells about four people who became nauseated and dizzy during a high school football game in California. The four all were found to have consumed soft drinks dispensed from a vending machine under the stadium stands. Authorities wondered if copper sulfate from pipes had infiltrated the water and contaminated the soft drinks. Or had the soft-drink syrup been contaminated by some bacteriological organisms or viruses?

The stadium had no loudspeaker system. So the authorities told the cheerleaders to announce that no one in the stands should consume any soft drinks from the vending machine until the cause of illness could be determined. No sooner had the cheerleaders made this appeal, however, than the entire stadium became a sea of retching, fainting spectators. A total of 191 persons were hospitalized. Subsequent laboratory analysis showed no contamination in the water or the soft drink syrup. Whatever the 191 spectators *caught*, it resulted from their minds telling their bodies they might be sick—and they were. It's all connected.

Such connections aren't always health oriented. Some are geographic—and economic. For example, Kaiser Steel shut down its iron mine in Eagle Mountain, California and ordered everyone out of the company town. While Japanese iron purchases had kept the small mining town alive in the past, the Japanese had decided that the Eagle Mountain iron was now too expensive. So they began to buy lower-priced iron from an Australian mining company instead, and Eagle Mountain's fate was sealed. The decision made in far-away Japan changed the lives of all of Eagle Mountain's 200 residents.

Everything Is Connected

The ultimate connection is fully understanding that each of us is one full unit of humanity, united with every other. We carry the information of our species deep in every cell. There, we have access to all of our own life information, and to everyone else's, if we but choose to realize it. As Walt Whitman said in *Leaves of Grass,*

> I CELEBRATE MYSELF. And what I
> assume you shall assume. For every atom
> belonging to me as good belongs to you.
> We are of each other. We are one.

Finding: The Observer Creates the Event

As noted earlier, people make their own reality. So do buffalo. If buffalo are herded into an area, you can erect a fence of mere burlap around them, and they'll stay penned in because they believe it to be solid and impenetrable.

Ralph Strauch, in his book, *The Reality Illusion,* illustrates how we humans make our own reality. Take a few moments and try it.

Hold your right hand in front of you. With your left hand, grasp your right wrist. Now try to raise your right hand, at the same time you hold it in place with your left. Do that long enough and hard enough so you can really feel your muscles. Notice the feeling of pushing that occurs in your wrists, arms, and shoulders. Also notice the feeling in your left hand and right wrist, and that most of the energy from both hands is concentrated at that point.

Do you feel as though you were pushing up hard with your right hand, and down with your left? If so, the two pushes cancel each other, causing you to feel stuck. No movement. No work done. Nothing realized.

Now do the same thing again. This time direct your attention away from the point of contact at the wrist, and concentrate on the muscles of your arm and shoulder. Sense the feeling in those muscles. Concentrate very hard on keeping them as they are—working against each other. Without changing anything in your right arm, release your hold. Now withdraw your left arm.

What happened to your right arm? Did it pop up because you released pressure on it, or did it stay stuck? It's reasonable to expect your arm would pop up. However, if you followed the directions and concentrated your mind on your right shoulder muscles, your right hand stayed right where it was.

Now try the same exercise again, this time concentrating your mind on the point of stress between your right wrist and left hand. Concentrate on the wrist, and let go with the left hand. Does your right hand pop up?

By now, I hope the lesson is clear. Your mind can create your own limitations or strengths. You do create your own reality.

When you know that life is uncertain, complementary, and connected, you suddenly realize that you have a lot more working for you than you thought. You begin to realize you don't have to strive as hard to *make it happen*. When you do, stop and ask yourself what you are doing and why. This doesn't mean you should sit around staring at blue-birds. It means you should actively do what gives you joy. Then you will feel whole, right, and full. Jim Haynes, in his book, *Workers of the World Unite and Stop Working,* calls this *fullering*.

We don't have to continually strive to grab the brass ring. We have it — it's Life.

When we know how life works in the micro-scopic world, we recognize that life works very sim-ilarly in our own. It helps us to trust *life* more. That doesn't mean it is easy, but it is easier. The new phys-ics, then, offers us an attitude about life. An attitude which tells us that life knows what it's doing and that it works—maybe not always the way we want it to, but it works. It helps us weather difficult times. And it gives us the opportunity to rejoice when things *fall together*, usually much to our surprise.

As we've seen, the new physics teaches us that life is complementary and uncertain—but, in this complementarity, everything is connected, the whole is *more* than the sum of its parts, and we do create our own reality. Knowing this, we realize that we don't have to try to grab the brass ring, we have it—it's Life.

5

LIFE IS A CONTINUAL S.O.S.
(Self-Organizing System)

Differences

Traditional career suggests control of life using goal setting
and planning. Lifecareer supports cooperation with
life, using the Career Compass for setting
intentions and organizing.

Life is a continuously self-organizing system
(SOS), and a more dependable one than most of us
imagine. That is, life organizes on its own, given its
inherent intelligence, even at the particle level. Our
cells, our organs, our body, the groups we are in, our
communities, states, nations, world, universe, and
even our *Lifecareers*—all are self-organizing systems. Now this doesn't necessarily mean we always
like the results. It merely means that self organization is built into life and is continually happening.
So, when we don't organize, life does it for us. And
even when we *do* organize, life often reorganizes

that, too.

Self organization is continuous because of life's
many fluctuations and disturbances. These cause
growth and change. Ilya Prigogine, who won a No-
bel prize in chemistry for his pioneering concept of
dissipative structures, describes them as "open systems that maintain their structure by continually ex-
changing energy with their environment." Prigogine
notes that fluctuation is the main process of all self
organization. Self-organizing living systems experience countless fluctuations. And periodically some of
these fluctuations are driven to their limits. This im-
balance is frequently called *stress.* During such im-
balance, either of two things may happen—mainte-
nance/renewal or growth. Since all living things
experience fluctuations, they're constantly striving
for balance by maintaining and growing. For instance, when you walk fast or run, your heart beats
more rapidly, and you begin to breathe faster. Then
when you stop, your breathing returns to normal. As
it resumes its normal rhythm, it is maintaining.

But, during periods of crisis, when you think
nothing is working—you've just gotten laid off or
divorced, or your business has failed—you try hard to
maintain balance, to retain your former equilibrium.
However, the fluctuations may be too great, and
instability results. Then you experience a period of
mental and/or physical uncertainty which can sur-
face in your body, your behavior, and/or your social
or professional relationships. You may be depressed,
restless, indecisive, have headaches or other physical
problems, and feel you're getting nowhere. You find
your energy is low; you need more sleep; and you
may not be as social as before. But, after a time, your
system reorganizes and you either maintain at a new
level or you reach a breakthrough.

In gaining this new state, you've grown and
learned. You're now different from what you were

and can reach a higher level of stability. This also is
true after experiencing a serious illness. People who
have done so say they're different from before.
They've grown, they've evolved. They feel healthier
than they did before the illness.

Sometimes the system can't adapt to such challenges. If it doesn't adapt to handle the change in energy, or adapt quickly enough, then it'll continue as
before or wither. Endless examples exist all around
us, in plants, people, cities, even whole nations. And,
for our purposes here, in *Lifecareer*.

Life's Disturbances and Reorganizations

Divorce

Everything comes apart (dissipates) and reorganizes continually. Fluctuation is the stuff of life.
You may not even be aware of it unless it's a major
event, such as having a serious illness or experiencing a romantic breakup *(dissipative structure)*,
as in the following example:

John and Sally have been married for fifteen
years. They have three children. One evening, after
returning home from the movies, John looks more
serious than usual. "Let's talk," he says.

"Okay." Sally has started undressing for bed.

John begins hesitantly. "I don't know how to tell
you this, but...I want a divorce."

"You *what*?" She turns and looks at him. "You're
not serious?"

The expression on his face tells her he is. "I'm in
love with someone else."

Sally is dumbstruck. "For God's sake, who is
she?"

"It doesn't matter." John shakes his head. "We've
been having an affair for twelve years, and I think
it's time I did something about it."

This is an example of a dissipative structure. Each life that this situation touches will be disturbed and reorganized. And each person it affects will have his or her own lessons to learn from it, including the opportunity to gain a new, higher level of growth.

Unemployment, Explosion, and Hijacking

Disturbance and dissipation can take many forms. Millions of unemployed persons, for example, are experiencing disturbance and reorganization in their lives, as they struggle to survive. Similarly, the eruption of Mount St. Helens not only changed the land, but also rearranged the lives of many people. Some were killed or injured. Others were emotionally shaken. Many moved away. But, life, the land, and the people continue. In a different type of disturbance, the passengers and crew members aboard TWA 847 hijacked on June 14, 1984 at the Athens airport by Shia Muslim terrorists had a startling disruption of their lives. Cities also experience major disturbances. In Baltimore, Maryland, the old downtown area is being rebuilt. Old, decaying buildings are being renovated and transformed into beautiful townhouses and condominiums. They are *dissipative structures*—moving from one form to another. So, you see, it isn't new to us. We know it. We live it.

Two Possibilities Always Exist: Maintenance/Renewal and Growth

Life offers us continuous opportunities to maintain and to grow. But we don't always pay much heed to some maintenance functions. For example, as Fritjof Capra points out in his book, *The Turning Point,* "The pancreas replaces most of its cells every 24 hours, the stomach lining every three days, our white blood cells renew in ten days, and 98 percent of the protein in the brain turns over in less than one month" (pp. 271-272). Yet, we hardly notice. And we still recognize our friends.

We also may not see opportunities for growth. For example, the growth opportunities that await us in what may appear to be a crisis—a sudden job loss, a serious illness, a romantic break-up, the death of a loved one. Each of these seeming crises has the potential to propel us into growth. Whether we'll act on it depends on whether we view it as adversity or opportunity and how trusting we are that our lives, like the cells in our bodies, are self organizing.

Since Life continually changes, reorganizing both humans and their environment, it may be useful to apply George Boole's idea of reduction from absurdity to your life direction problem. That is, jump in, do the most absurd thing and work your way to what you want through successive approximations.

When society unleashes change on us that's too great for us to absorb, we're forced to reorganize. When our familiar structures start to disappear, we're forced to go beyond our former limits. We wonder if we can press through to a new level or not. Could the old-fashioned horse and buggy really give way to the motor car? It has—remarkably. And we each can advance to a new and more comprehensive personal level. We do it every day—we just don't realize it.

Consider those persons who are having to remake how they earn their livings. Today, many jobs

once considered important to our nation's economy
are moving abroad, are being lost to foreign competition, or are being replaced by robots or computers.
Television tubes, pacemakers, and even steel are being produced overseas by American firms. General
Electric, for example, shut down its iron-making
plant in Ontario, California and moved its production
to Singapore, displacing some 1,000 workers. In the
telephone and telecommunications industries, computers have eliminated 100,000 jobs. And the intro-
duction of home banking in just one area of northern
California in 1984 caused the layoff of some 5,000
bank employees.

As corporate directors give closer scrutiny to
their balance sheets and bottom lines, the chances for
dissipation and the reorganization of goals and personnel greatly increase. If you realize that life is continually changing (dissipating) and reorganizing,
then, whatever happens in your life, you expect. As a
result, when a sudden shift happens in your life, you
don't plunge into a deep depression.

When you expect change, you no longer depend
on your employer to take care of you. You know
there are no guarantees, that your main security is
your ability to make a living, to move to another job,
or to create your own work. Security on your present
job is merely wishful thinking, an illusion. If you
come to work one day to find the office or plant
closed—or gone altogether—that's the way it is. In
fact, that's exactly what happened to 750 employees
of the Joseph Magnin stores when they appeared for
work on September 18, 1984. They discovered they
no longer had jobs. The Joseph Magnin organization
had closed all 24 of its stores and filed a bankruptcy
petition. Don't be complacent and tell yourself that it
can't happen to you. Anyone working for someone
else is subject to this possibility. Atlantic Richfield
Corporation recently announced a major financial

restructuring that will lay off thousands of employees and force many into early retirement. So, change and reorganization is the name of the game for all.

"Ah," you say, "I'm a member of a top law firm, and top law firms don't shut down." They do if all their business moves out. Or if motorists decide to quit suing over every bumper-thumper accident. Or if law schools spawn potential lawyers in the ever-increasing numbers they are today. Remember, it's all connected. Some law firms are already offering fast, easy, low-cost service, like fast-food chains. They're even opening offices in former Pizza Hut locations and giving their competitors a run for their money. Nothing is for certain, but it's all connected.

This can be seen in the long-term dissipation and reorganization that showed up in our shift from an agricultural to an industrial society. Since the change and reconstruction came about slowly over time, many weren't consciously aware of the change and how it organized itself into a new era: the Industrial Age. At the peak of the earlier agricultural period, 95 percent of our nation's people lived and worked on the land, supporting both themselves and the city dwellers. Today, fewer than 5 percent of all Americans make their living directly from agriculture—yet they feed and clothe the rest of the population, with an abundance left over.

The transition brought about by the Industrial Revolution was from farm to factory, but look at the factories now. Timothy Wirth, Former Chairman, House Subcommittee on Telecommunications, noted in the mid-1980s that only 13 percent of the American work force manufactures products; 87 percent does something else. The conclusion is clear. We're not just thinking about moving out of manufacturing. We've already done it.

Today, we're witnessing the restructuring of still another new era: the post-industrial period. The major transition now under way is from *factory / products* to *thoughts / words*. This is reorganizing our economy and changing the occupational structure. This will eventually shake up and reorganize our entire educational system. Note that when one thing changes, everything connected to it changes. And today, we're learning just how connected everything is.

If you don't experience tremors in the organization you work for or in your social relationships, you're bound to experience them in your own personal growth. Louise, at age 29, was earning $48,000 a year at her job and receiving generous fringe benefits. She had grown dissatisfied, however. She wanted to do something more creative—and challenging. She also wanted to continue at the same earnings level or higher. In time, however, Louise became willing to forgo a handsome salary and fringe benefits in order to satisfy her growth needs. She began to explore various fields and found that she enjoyed fashion merchandising. She found it stimulating and exciting. Louise will start to train for a job in that field soon. But, for now, she plans to retain her present job until she feels the transition is right for her.

The World View Shift—A Reorganization of Our Perspective

The notion that life is neat, simple, stable, machine-like, and predictable is causing fluctuations and reorganization in many lives today. You might call it a *mindquake*.

We're all experiencing mindquakes and attitude shifts at some level. When the dust settles, we find we're stronger for the experience. It does no good to wish away the changes, to deny them, or to ignore them. Change has always happened, and it always will. As noted earlier, if you recognize them, crisis and change provide the opportunity for rebuilding and growth. Larry Dossey, M.D. observes in his book *Space, Time, and Medicine* that structures insulated from disturbance are protected from change.

Life at the cell level is self organizing, so are our Lifecareers.

Change is integral in all forms of life. Life forms are characterized by their potential for self-renewal (ability to renew and recycle atoms, cells, organs, and parts) and their capacity to reach beyond their mental and physical boundaries. By acknowledging these abilities, we gain new faith in our healing and our joy in becoming more than we are. We then understand that Lifecareer is:

- uncertain, and connected to everything;
- complementarity at work; and
- constantly bringing order out of chaos.

Through its instability, your Lifecareer is continually being given the opportunity to improve and move into greater complexity. Its whole is more than the sum of its parts. Your Lifecareer informs you that it is you forever remaking your own world—setting new intentions, shedding your limitations. **It is you realizing that, just as life at the cell level is self organizing, your *Lifecareer* also is self organizing.** Continue to ask yourself, "How do I feel and what shall I do about what I'm feeling?" You have all your answers.

PART II

LIVING LIFECAREER

6

LIFE-AS-CAREER: LETTING GO

Differences

Traditional career suggests that one needs to find the way
before letting go. In Lifecareer, one lets go, then
discerns direction.

Finding Your New Direction
and the Letting Go

Should you wait until you've found something
else before letting go of what you have? Many people
think you should. "It's just common sense," they say.
And you'll feel more secure that way. Yet, letting go
offers its own feelings of security and certainty. And
freely finding your way isn't easy when you cling to
old structures and outmoded thought patterns. Besides, when you let go, you're not without an anchor.
You have your experience, intelligence, and intuition
to guide you. Then you truly know where your personal power is.

Assumptions Worth Examining
in Letting Go

As we've seen, the universe is an infinite, inter-dependent system. A system can't function without some of its parts. When all its parts work together, the system operates. This is true of solar systems, of corporations, of atoms, of clocks, and of humans.

So, when I speak of letting go, it doesn't mean you should try to let go of the parts of you essential to your functioning, such as experience, intelligence, intuition, wisdom, faith, feelings, courage, confidence. These are elements that help you grow. Rather, it means abandoning old ideas and faulty assumptions you've invented, carried around, and practiced for so long you may not realize that they're old and faulty.

Such ideas and assumptions are directly linked to your behavior and attitudes. And these, in turn, can affect your body and mind in hurtful, hazardous ways. Faulty behavior and attitudes, for example, signal your body, "Something may be wrong—tense up!" This is called *stress*.

Releasing old ideas and faulty assumptions is the psychological equivalent of eliminating bodily wastes—both serve to keep us cleansed and healthy. The problem is that the mind is much less inclined or sometimes less able to let go of such wastes than is the body. In this regard, the body has a superior technology. The mind tries to retain everything forever. Our minds, for example, don't advance into adulthood automatically. They stay adolescent until something prods and moves them on. One way we can mature is to identify and discard those ideas and assumptions that no longer serve us.

Let's look at several assumptions that tend to keep us from fully living *Life*-as-career.

Does Reality Exist?

The first assumption worth examining is that *reality* exists. *Reality* is what *you* think it is. It's only *your* conception. How often have you heard it said, "She doesn't know what it's *really* like..." Or "Come on, let's be *realistic*...." Who can say what's realistic for another person? Even when you and I experience *the same thing*, what it's like for you is different from what it's like for me.

Our realities of the same event, then, are different. Why? Because each of us makes our own reality. Every moment of our lives, we each see and feel and live the *reality* around us consistent with how we individually perceive it. The philosophy of pragmatism suggests that the mind deals only with ideas, therefore, the mind can only ponder its ideas about reality. In his book *The Dancing Wu Li Masters,* Gary Zukav notes that even the scientists have found that a complete understanding of reality lies beyond the capabilities of rational thought. Have you ever been in a group of people who saw a traffic accident? Did any two of them agree on what happened? Most of the time, you can depend on each account being just a little different.

Quantum theory laid to rest the old notion that objectivity is possible. Zukav notes:

> According to quantum mechanics, there is no such thing as objectivity. We cannot eliminate ourselves from the picture. We are a part of nature, and when we study nature there is no way around the fact that nature is studying itself (p. 56).

If you want good reality, then make good reality. After all, what's real is only your perception of it. You find what you look for. And you get what you think about. Moreover, what you look for largely depends on what you've found formerly. It's like the Easterner and the Westerner driving through Arizona

one night and spotting a large tumbleweed ahead on
the road. The Easterner grows excited: he thinks
they're going to hit a boulder. The Westerner smiles.
He knows it's a tumbleweed. You're conditioned by
what you're used to perceiving.

Our tendency to decide what's *real* or *realistic*
for others also grows out of this faulty assumption. A
teacher tells a student, "You don't know what the real
world is like." What the teacher is saying is, "I know,
you don't." To make matters worse, many people
who speak of the *real world* aren't speaking as much
from personal experience as from prejudices, hear-
say, misperceptions, faulty beliefs, or misinformed
judgments.

What counselors usually mean when they tell
their clients, "That's not realistic" is "You haven't
experienced your choice." But, frequently, neither
has the counselor. One reality, then, is as good as the
other. And we all do better when we learn through
experience.

The first step is to *let go* of the need to tell others
what is *realistic*. The second step is to realize that
what we tell others has more to do with our own issues than it does with their possibilities.

Is the Self Lost?

The second assumption worth examining is that
the self is somehow lost and needs finding.

We all generally know who we are most of the
time. But who we are changes, evolves, fades in and
out of consciousness, as we seek to keep up with it.
New information about who we are bombards us
continually. We may not acknowledge it, but change
is happening. As soon as we've experienced a major
event or transition, we need to examine how we
emerge from it, to learn who the *new* us is.

Further, we don't have to wait until we *know*
who we *are* to act. It's in the acting that we learn

more about ourselves. If we sit alone in our rooms and contemplate *who* we *are,* the moment we emerge to face the world, we become different from what we were in isolation.

Thinking we need to find ourselves suggests that we're lost. And losing ourselves just isn't possible. For better or worse, we have ourselves for life.

What's needed, instead of thinking our self is lost, is acknowledgement that we know as much as we can in the minute. But we need to keep learning more about ourselves now, days, weeks, months, and years from now, for the rest of our lives. Information about who we are fills our *in-basket* of life. And we have to keep examining that information to stay current on who we are. We can ignore it, but it'll continue accumulating. It may soon spill over and overwhelm us. That's usually when we think we don't know who we are and that we need to find ourselves.

Keep in mind—you never complete yourself. You constantly add to the information you have about yourself. And it replaces, updates, rearranges all previous information. This is the *dissipative structures* idea discussed in Chapter 5. From change comes growth. Out of chaos emerges pattern and order.

Battered and Abused Careers: Fact or Fiction?

Often, our career goals or aspirations are abused by people who tell us that we have no experience, that we're not suited, or that what we want isn't realistic. They say this in such a polite, acceptable way that we're apt to think they're right. This makes us distrust our own inner knowing, our instincts, our intuition. If people—especially young people—hear such things often enough from counselors, teachers, or other authority figures, they start to believe them. They gradually shut down their inner drives. They stop having faith in themselves. They become disheartened.

Each of us knows better than anyone else what we want. We alone have all our personal information. We serve as our own full-time biographers, historians, knowers of what we need and what we want. As e.e. cummings observed in *A Poet's Advice:*

> To be nobody but yourself—in a world
> that is doing its best, night and day, to
> make you everybody else—means to fight
> the hardest battle which any human being
> can fight and never stop fighting.

Is There a Graceful Way to Be Presumptuous?

A counselor recently asked: "How can you gracefully tell someone that he or she isn't capable of handling the career he or she has chosen, and yet not destroy that person's enthusiasm?" You can't—because you're challenging that person's *reality*—laying your reality on them.

Don't stumble over things behind you.

Let's start instead by pointing out that everyone has a career. This the counselor didn't do in asking that question. If you have life, you have a career. A valuable, important career. Tell your counselees that *life* is career. Tell them to focus on life and see what job possibilities occur to them. Give them the feeling of starting with something. With this knowledge of already having a career comes the responsibility that goes with it. Hence, they're able to explore livelihood possibilities knowing they have a good foundation, instead of feeling they never have enough and everything is always out there—out of their reach.

Next, telling someone he or she can't do a specific job is presumptuous. It can damage the person's self-image. And it's a world apart from allowing the person to find out for him or herself. That's experience in action. That's learning how to read your experience and know the next step.

Let the person collect such information through experience. Insist upon it. The person will learn very quickly whether he or she's suited for the job and wants to follow it as a work-career. None of us needs to hear we aren't capable. We need to learn, through experience, what we can and can't do.

People who try to gracefully tell others their limitations believe they're doing the right thing.They may even think they're saving the person time. A large part of our career counseling system today is based on this unfortunate notion. It can seriously damage our self-esteem. And consider how many different opportunities we already have in life to get our self-esteem thumped.

Is There a Top to Reach?

The third assumption that warrants examination is that there's a *top* to reach.

Do you want to be free? Then release the idea that there's a top. When everything's connected, where's the top?

The people who are happy are those whose circumstances are good relative to the standards they set for themselves.

The top that you strive and study and struggle to reach is probably what your friends or associates *think* is the top. Why let others define your life direction? If you must strive to reach the top, define what it is yourself—and how to reach it. Someone else's top simply won't work for you. You can never, never reach it. It's like a shell game. It's never where you think it is.

Next, save your energy for your own trip. Don't try to take someone else's trip. And when you start working toward your intentions, be aware that life is full of surprises, some of them painful and sad while others are fun and exciting.

Lastly, don't spend today focusing on a long-gone yesterday. Don't back through life rear-end first, gazing at yesterday and worrying about what tomorrow may level at your exposed backside. Instead, live in the present and watch it unfold for you. Act using your Career Compass (your experience, intelligence and intuition).

Dr. Allen Parducci offers this observation on happiness and the *top* we pick for ourselves:

> ...a lot of money, great looks, a splendid economy, enormous intelligence and peace on earth are not things that determine our happiness or unhappiness. Instead...people who are happy are people whose circumstances are good relative to the standards they set for themselves (p. 4).

If you set moderate intentions for yourself, you may find it much easier to be happy than if you set overly high expectations. Maybe this explains why an old backwoods gent appears happy rocking in a chair on the porch of his rickety shack while some wealthy, jet-set celebrities in the fast lane of life never seem happy. Their goals may outreach their ability to get them. And for some of us, the harder we run, the farther away the finish line becomes. That makes for a difficult, frustrating race.

A Mistake or a Mis Take?

The fourth assumption that needs examining is your attitude about mistakes—or your fear of making them.

Let go of the idea of mistakes. Society will tell you that making a mistake is doing something wrong. But, you learn from mistakes. You learn *what* to do and not do. You learn that a mistake is part of the going-forward process. And if you can learn from it, then it can't be a mistake.

For example, in film-making, a *mis take* is a scene that didn't go quite as the director wanted. But, film people learn from these *mis takes*. Sometimes, *mis takes* are even used in the finished film, not because they're right, but because they work. They're more effective than the intended scene.

Can Time Be *Wasted*?

The final area worth examining is your attitude about the time you give yourself—and the common assumption that we should use time productively, not waste it.

All time is used productively. None is wasted. Let go of the notion that just *hanging out* is wasted time. A college student recently told me that when he had felt depressed earlier that day, he walked around the campus until he felt better. "I wasted the whole afternoon," he said. In the academic climate in which he lives, any time that's not devoted to attending classes or studying is regarded by many as wasted. Yet, walking around, thinking, and trying to get oneself up is anything but wasted time—it's time spent taking care of yourself. And *who* matters more? You needn't charge through life, filling every moment with visibly productive activity. You needn't be an automaton.

However, you *do* need to make time periodically

to review what you're doing, to organize, and to listen to your Career Compass. This calls for occasionally just sitting and thinking. Or sit and stare. Or play an instrument simply because you enjoy it. Go for a walk. Take a nap. None of these is wasted time. Allow your lower and higher levels of consciousness to rest and regenerate. They'll serve you better.

Further, only *you* are qualified to determine that you're wasting time. If you feel uneasy about how you're spending some of your time, then get moving and do something you consider productive. Or fire your *thinker* for making you feel you're wasting time. Or work on your focus, work on your self-discipline, work on your willpower. Make sure you're not feeling needlessly guilty.

Do Things Right or Do Right Things?

Another point worth considering is this: is it more important to *do things right* or to *do right things?* Think about that for a moment.

In the recent book *Leaders: Strategies for Taking Charge,* Warren Bennis describes the findings of his study of leading corporate executives and their leadership styles. Bennis found that good leaders *do right things,* and that good managers *do things right.* For example, good leaders focus on using the strengths of their subordinates, *not* on correcting their weaknesses. Good self-leadership similarly calls for putting our personal strengths to work—not lamenting our weaknesses. Most of us could fill volumes on our weaknesses. Good self-leadership also calls for *doing right things*—that is, doing what each of us thinks is right for *us* instead of trying to *do things right* (that is, what others think is right).

Is Losing Your Job a Bad Thing?

Also worth considering is how you feel when

you lose a job. Let go of the notion that losing a job is a crisis. True, it's not fun. It even may be scary. But, often it ends up as an opportunity. Many people better themselves when they have to seek new jobs or to create their own work. The rewards may range from learning new skills or earning more money to having the chance to meet interesting people or moving to an exciting new place. Flip the coin of crisis, and you'll find opportunity on the other side. Even the current trend among our nation's industrial companies to move their assembly-line operations to other countries has opened opportunities to many company executives who have lost their jobs.

Top executives, along with the workers, are experiencing crisis in career. These executives are toppling from their six-figure positions. Often, they're lucky to have a job when their company suddenly pulls out to set up in a labor-cheap location. Many secure middle-managers join the ranks of the unemployed, finding themselves side by side with the former assembly-line workers they managed. A recent survey showed that jobless executives in the $40,000 to $60,000 bracket seemed to have the hardest time finding new employment. Those in the bracket below $40,000 or above $60,000 found new positions in an average of 14.5 weeks while middle level executives took 21 weeks. Surprise! Most all the new jobs paid an average of 20 percent more than the previous jobs.

Living Life Flexibly Is Important

As employees watch their jobs move to other countries or become gobbled up by modernization, they learn to rethink their lives. They learn to be flexible. They come to discard old myths about work and education and to establish new truths. We'll discuss more about this later.

Today, computerization is displacing thousands

of workers, forcing them to turn inward to find answers about their lives. In one Japanese factory, for
example, three men at computer terminals control
robots that are the primary work force for the 54,000
square foot plant. Ninety-seven workers maintain the
machining cells of these robots. The plant reportedly
is five times more productive than its conventional
counterpart would be.

The inability of today's computer technicians to
operate tomorrow's more advanced computers may
make their jobs obsolete as well. These new-genera-
tion computers also can be expected to swallow up
large numbers of secretarial and other office positions. Graphics, engineering, and telecommunication
jobs continue to be computerized, hence eliminating
workers. What do you do when this happens? Where
will you go if you're displaced?

My bank manager recently said, "Within five
years, you'll walk into a bank and see only four or
five employees. Everything is being centralized. Our
bank is currently training its managers to be sales
people. We're going to be selling bank services door
to door. Those of us who don't want to sell are already looking around for other work, because it's
now under way." While he had thought that being a
bank manager would give him an inside managerial
job, his position is now being transformed into an
outside selling job.

For reasons like these, more and more people today are joining the ranks of the unemployed. Many
of them will be forced to earn their income from
multiple sources. Some will turn to working at home,
producing products or supplying services—today an
income source for some 18 million people nationwide.

As we've seen, then, losing or deciding to leave
your job needn't create a crisis. It can turn into opportunity when you decide to let go of the crisis side

and see the problem as an opportunity.

A Rest Please

Maybe you're thinking, "But I can't discard all my faulty beliefs and perceptions immediately. I've relied on them for so long—I'd feel lost." If so, take heart. You needn't discard them all immediately. Do it gradually, like this: jot down on a piece of paper any faulty beliefs you have had. Then put the list aside, where you can find it easily. Each time another faulty belief comes to mind that you want to eliminate, add it to the list. Then, when the time is right (and you'll know when), flush or burn the list—but get rid of it.

Should We Let Go of Planning?

Most of us have been taught that planning isn't only important, it's essential. There's a phrase in business that goes something like this: "If you fail to plan, you plan to fail." This statement needs careful examination.

Whatever works is the plan — so there's no such thing as the plan not working.

Let's agree that we all do short-term planning. This type of planning usually is flexible. If what we plan for the day doesn't work out, we accept it and do something else. Aside from flexible planning, most of us make fixed plans. That is, we make advance appointments with a doctor or the dentist. Or we reserve travel accommodations ahead.

Today, however, we find ourselves forced into more and more flexible planning because things are changing too rapidly to fit plans. This means making faster and more decisions. Since it takes energy to

make decisions, we sometimes grow tired and just
put our decisions on hold. Change, however, is still
happening. Some event or situation forces us to make
another flexible plan, right on the heels of our former
one. This need for spontaneous, flexible planning is
somewhat new to us. Most of us are accustomed to
our plans holding for longer periods of time, as they
did in earlier years when things were more stable,
secure, and slower-paced.

Because flexible planning calls for quick reaction, we find ourselves relying more on our experience, intelligence, and intuition, and less on fixed
plans. We're not used to that either. But, we know
that both fixed and flexible planning strategies are
helpful in living *Life*-as-career, just as night and day
are beneficial in giving us time to rest and time for
activity. Flexible planning, however, enables us to
change course as we wish. For example, a young
fashion model with a great wish to travel thought
that getting a degree in journalism would lead her to
a travel-oriented job. So she enrolled in college, ma-
joring in journalism. After her first year in school, she
received a call from a New York film producer. He
had seen her face on a billboard and asked her to test
for the lead role in a documentary film he was producing.

Since her plans were flexible, she tested for the
role, got it, and left college. When the film was finished, she stayed on in New York City to study acting. This work-career choice enabled her to travel.

You'll find endless examples like this of people
living the flexible plan. If we took a survey, we'd
probably find that most people plan flexibly—but we
sometimes don't realize it. Instead, we're apt to criti-
cize ourselves for not having a plan or for not moving forward. The important questions to ask are: "Am
I following what seems right at the moment?" and
"Do I feel good about where I'm heading?" Make

sure that your flexible planning is getting you where
you want to go. If it isn't, you may want to rethink
what you're doing.

Living *Life*-as-career means continual change
and movement. Because it does, we want to keep
ourselves free to act spontaneously. This means not
having our minds set so firmly on a plan that we
can't change direction. It used to be that people who
didn't have a set plan and moved around were called
shiftless. Now we realize that people who *hang loose*
are flexible and have the *real* edge. They're not con-
strained by a fixed, rigid plan. They're free to move
forward.

Using the *Intention* Approach

Planning is healthy, when we live our plans
flexibly and creatively. Rational (fixed) planning also
has its place. For example, planning for new schools
to prepare a construction budget, or targeting consumer markets to sell a new product—these and similar situations need fixed planning. However, be
cautious. Don't lock your *Lifecareer* into a fixed, rigid
plan. And don't chide yourself for not having a *Lifecareer* master plan or for abandoning any such plan
you've made.

---

*When my intentions are one with the
rhythm of life, the answers manifest
quickly. When they're not, the answers
just plain won't unfold.*

Instead, if you plan, combine fixed and flexible
planning, with *more* flexible than fixed. My fixed
planning, for example, includes scheduling time for
appointments, teaching commitments, lectures, and
seminars. The remaining time is left flexible for any

needs, wants, or activities that may arise. As for long-range planning, I mostly just set *intentions* about what I want to do in life. I have a general idea of what I want to do, but I may be uncertain *how* to do it. I may even be downright perplexed about where to start. In other words, I have no step-by-step plan for carrying out my intention. I'm comfortable with that because my experience has taught me that, once I set the intention and begin to seriously follow my experience, intelligence, and intuition, the *what* and the *how* unfold—they show themselves to me as I open myself to them. Sometimes this happens quickly, other times it takes longer. For example, when my intentions are one with the rhythm of life, the answers manifest quickly. When they're not, the answers just plain won't unfold.

Once you've set your intention, simply go about your life.

Once you've set your intention, the next step is simply to go about your life. You may soon find yourself getting ideas and answers from diverse sources—from people you talk with, items you read, programs you attend, and so on. You also may receive answers from your subconscious if you direct your mind to work on them.

As these answers begin to come to you, you'll suddenly become aware of them. You didn't sit down and rationally turn up answers. Instead, you set your intention, went about your normal everyday activities, and what you needed found its way to you. Too, you put very little energy into finding answers. That's the way it works. When you set an intention, keep it uppermost in your mind, stay open to all incoming information, and do what feels right in the moment. You may be surprised at how effortlessly answers form around it. By using this approach, you'll save on the energy normally spent in going over why things haven't worked as planned. When you set an intention, whatever works *is* the plan—so there's *no* such thing as the plan *not* working.

One Fixed Planning Technique— My *GLANCE* List

As part of my fixed planning, I jot down things I want to do on a *glance list*. Then, I periodically glance at this list. I don't regard these items as *musts*. They're merely things that seemed quite important when I wrote them. Sometimes *glancing* does me as much good as *doing* something on the list. My *glance list* also helps me to keep track of those things I want to get done. Sometimes it serves as something I can simply look at, then ignore. And that feels good, too.

The difference between a glance list and a must-do list is the difference between low stress and high stress.

Most mornings, I glance at the items on the list, consider my physical energy and well-being (I have low blood sugar and if my body isn't balanced that determines how much I choose to do), check out my mood, check out my Career Compass—my experience, intelligence, and intuition—then decide my priorities for the day. The difference between a *glance list* and a *must-do* list is the difference between low stress and high stress. *Glance* is an act, *must* is a command, and I try not to *must* myself. Added to this, I don't rationally set priorities. I let

them make themselves known to me. Then I act on
them. This approach seems to work well for me. I
don't sit and ponder what my next priority is. Instead, I let it unfold—and go from there. Try it. See
how it works for you.

Do You Need a Master Plan
for Your Life?

When your *Lifecareer* is on the flexible plan, you
let go of the notion that you have to chart a master
plan for your life. Remember, rational (fixed) planning is a technique that was first introduced to increase output on factory assembly lines, where it
proved useful for that purpose. After all, a box of
Wheaties doesn't move unless workers get it down
the assembly line and en route to your store by a certain time. But, lives aren't boxes of Wheaties. They
don't sit in one place until moved (though one might
argue that some people seem to do little more).

We all continually experience what Buckminster
Fuller called a *precession effect*. To illustrate what
this means, consider this: when a bumblebee dips into
a flower to extract honey, its wings brush the pollen.
Then when it dips into the next flower, it leaves some
pollen gathered from the previous flowers. The result
is cross-fertilization of the flowers. What seemed like
a side effect in one instance has become a main effect
in another. You and I are similarly moving, connect-
ing beings who continually bump into different
people, different situations. We experience this
change and that change, unaware that something
which seems trivial then might become very significant. We leave a little Lifecareer pollen here, pick up
a little there. We've all experienced bumping into
someone who later could help us in some way. Or the
reverse may be true—we have the opportunity to
help someone else. That's the wonder and beauty of
our journeys as humans.

Just as rational planning must combine with flexible planning to gain positive change in our lives, so Roger Harrison of the consulting firm of Harrison, Kouzes Associates questions whether rational planning alone can be used to effect change in organizations:

> In fact, I have never in all my years as a consultant seen anyone change an organization in any fundamental way by rational planning. Plans have their place, of course, but the managers I have seen change their organization's character always operated by intuition, guided by strongly-held intentions. They communicated their intentions verbally to others who could share their vision, and they communicated it daily to others through their real time actions and decisions. In due course, enough people shared the vision/ intention for it to reach 'critical mass,' and the dream became reality (p. 15).

In a similar way, we can *intend* what we want into becoming a reality in our lives.

Should You Make Long-Range Plans?

One of the few times you'll have to discuss long-range plans is on a job interview. A favorite question of most job interviewers is: "What are your long-range plans?" (A good answer that few can argue with is: "I plan to be intelligent in each moment.")

Do you have long-range plans? Do your friends and relatives? Ask them. Their answers may surprise you. At first, they may think you mean long-range job plans. But, when you clarify that *Lifecareer* means long-range *life* plans, chances are they'll be stymied. That's because many people think of *career* as job.

Your friends and relatives may have only vague ideas about how to get where they want to go. They may have short-range plans. But, most of us don't even make short-range plans. We make daily plans. We decide what we'll do day-by-day. That's the way most of us live our lives. We want our tomorrow to be better than today. But, that's about as specific as we get. And that's all right. We each have to do what we have to do. Even those who advocate rational planning probably find themselves living the short-range plan or the even shorter daily plan. The important question is, "Does it work?" If so, then why worry?

Life is what happens while we're busy planning.

Fritjof Capra, author of *The Turning Point*, keynoted *The 1983 Assembly to Advance Career*. He mentioned the pragmatic attitude in physics. "When you have a certain theory and you think it isn't quite mathematically sound or for some other reason you know it isn't a sound theory, but it works, it explains experiments, then you say, 'Well, there must be something to it.' If it works you'll use it and elaborate on it later." So, if life is working, simply go with it—and explain it later. That's what most of us do anyway.

When former President Reagan's son, Ronald, left the Joffrey Ballet in New York, he told those who asked what he planned to do next, "No, I haven't (decided) and I can't really tell you when I'll make a decision. I'll make a decision—when I decide, I suppose."

That's the way most of us make a decision—

when it's necessary. Or when we feel it's time to do so. We summon up strength from deep within and take the step, and it works. If we don't like how it works, we decide again.

CBS correspondent Jane Bryant Quinn, observes:

> When people say: 'you must plan your life, decide what you want in five years,' that's corporate thinking. If you try to impose that type of planning on creative careers, it doesn't work. I don't know a single woman writer or editor who sat down and said, 'In four years, that's where I want to be.' (1982)

We know that life is moving, active. We describe the universe, for example, in terms of waves and particles that move at the speed of light. In its continuous movement, life is ever changing, turbulent, seemingly chaotic—yet again and again coming into pattern. Then, as quickly, it falls out of pattern. If we combine flexible planning with fixed planning, then we find that our planning parallels the nature of the universe—unfolding.

It's also important to note that those who make long-range plans and follow through religiously often fare no better than those who approach life randomly and meet change as it comes. The important thing isn't which way you do it—plan your life completely or not at all—but to allow yourself *choices* about how you do it, doing what seems right for you. In summary, rigid, unswerving adherence to long-range goals can set you up for a terrible fall. When your plans don't materialize because your life and the world has changed, you may be a candidate for the screaming academy.

The Thing to Fear Is...

Now we come to fear, the bugaboo that prevents many of us from letting go, changing our courses, and taking up a new direction. If we're to move forward, letting go of fear is essential. Let's take a look at how to do that.

Face It—And Admit It

Next time you're faced with a frightening experience, listen for your inner being to call out, "But, I'm *scared!*" Check yourself for the signs of fear: feeling of anxiety or frustration, cramps, a headache, general aches all over, fatigue, shortness of breath, rapid pulse, clammy hands, rapid heartbeat, dry mouth, shortness of temper, twitches. Remember, our bodies are often the channel through which our minds and our emotions express themselves. We are a system—every single cell is linked in one way or another to every other. We are also a self-organizing system. Any negative energy unleashed in one area of our bodies in some way affects every other. Negative energy doesn't go away, it seeps into our tissues and muscles. It circulates in our blood streams. We rapidly become the type of energy we feel. Keep in mind—everything's connected.

How Do You Rate?

Fears are patient chameleons. They may hide from us for years. They can even take on the colors of our environments. Often, we don't know—or have forgotten—that we have a specific fear of something. Here's an easy way to measure your fears. Using a pencil, place a check in front of each statement that applies to you. Answer honestly. Then review your answers to see how you rate when it comes to fear.

1. When you attend a function where you don't know what the proper dress is, do you fear:
   ___ looking out of place?
   ___ being talked about or laughed at?
   ___ not blending in with the crowd?

2. If you're thinking about going back to school do you fear:
   ___ failure?
   ___ not fitting in?
   ___ that someone will think you're too old to be in school?

3. If you're in the business world, do you fear:
   ___ not making it with the *old boys*?
   ___ not doing things right?
   ___ making presentations?
   ___ not working long enough hours?
   ___ not being promoted?
   ___ someone being put ahead of you?
   ___ someone making a better impression?

4. If you're a teacher, do you fear:
   ___ you won't attract students?
   ___ your classes won't fill?
   ___ your colleagues won't like or think highly of you?
   ___ your colleagues will get more consulting work than you?
   ___ you won't get your share of department monies?
   ___ you won't get a merit raise?
   ___ that someone else will be brought into the department and reduce your chances for tenure?

5. In social situations, do you fear:
   ___ talking with the *wrong* people?

___ inviting the wrong mix of people to
    dinner?
___ not returning dinner invitations?
___ whether your home looks just right for
    guests?
___ whether what you serve will meet your
    guests' expectations?
___ whether you'll say something that may
    offend?

6. During a job interview, do you fear:
    ___ not being presently employed?
    ___ not being qualified?
    ___ being too old?
    ___ being a minority member?
    ___ not making a good impression on
        the interviewer?

7. If you're thinking about starting your own
    business, do you fear:
    ___ not making a living?
    ___ not being able to sell your product or
        service?
    ___ not knowing how to start?
    ___ that people won't help you?
    ___ not being able to attract customers?
    ___ running out of money?
    ___ not knowing where to find a
        business support group?

8. If you've just gotten a new job, do you fear:
    ___ not being able to do the work?
    ___ not liking your job?
    ___ not getting promoted?
    ___ being laid off or fired?
    ___ you won't quit, even if you grow
        bored with the job?

Now that you've finished the questions, go over

your answers. Each time you've checked a fear—no matter how vague or small—think about it. Where did that fear come from? Why do you have it? What does it *do* for you? Some of us hold on to fears to protect ourselves from something—failure, mistakes—or even success.

Keep in mind—fear isn't real, although the feeling surely is. If you approach each fear, squarely confront it, and deal with it, you'll find it's an illusion. A ghost. You made it up and then lived in fear of the fear you invented. Once you know this—and your reasons for doing so—you can begin to let go of it.

Just Let Go

Should You Rely on a Single Source for Your Income?

Increasingly, all of us will have to let go of the idea of earning our incomes from a single job or other source. This *one-job* tradition originated during the Industrial Revolution. "Come work for us full-time" beckoned the early mills and mines and sweat-shops, "and we'll pay you a living wage." Some even supplied their workers on-site company housing so they wouldn't have to spend time commuting to work. That was single-source full-time employment on a large scale, and it's carried over to today. Though single-source income no longer works for many of us, we aren't willing to release the idea too easily.

Many employers need full-time, 8-hour-a-day employees. Full-time labor is the Western way. Maybe you're thinking, "Yes, but I want a full-time not a part-time job." Then look for that full-time job, but you may have to settle for part-time work and creating a work of your own. The new work pattern in America is working for someone else while doing something yourself. Recently, it was reported that 46 percent of the college students defined success as owning their own business, so entrepreneuring is gaining popularity fueled by new technologies and the wish for more personal growth and creativity.

Another option would be to work only, say, four hours a day at your present job—then take a class or two at a nearby school to satisfy your learning needs. You might even go on to work for a couple of hours at another part-time job. Or what if you worked in your home for four hours a day, making a product or producing a service—then spent four hours a day working at something altogether different on a company job? You would then be living the new work-career pattern: piecing together your income from multiple sources. Would you rather work fewer hours, come and go more as you please, do an interesting variety of things during your workday, and still earn as much as or *more* than you do now? After all, that's a full-time life.

In summary, think about what you might want to let go of. Circle the following questions you want to think more about:

1. Should I hold on to what I have until I get something else in hand?
2. Does reality exist?
3. Is the self lost?
4. Is there a top to reach?
5. Is there such a thing as mistakes?
6. Can time be wasted?
7. Is losing a job an opportunity?
8. Should I plan?
9. Do I need a master plan for my life?
10. Are long-range goals helpful? Long-range plans?
11. Is it wise to rely on single source income?

Finally, make up your own list of things you might want to let go.

7

LIFE-AS-CAREER: FINDING YOUR WAY

Differences

Traditional career suggests that *knowing* where you're going
is a first condition in getting there. In Lifecareer
knowing is an on-going process and
comes with action.

Ready

The longer I work with Lifecareer, the more I
realize that finding one's way tends to come after letting go. That is, letting go of the idea that you need to
take your reading from someone else's Career Compass. When you do that, you're buying into someone
else's mythology, someone else's way of seeing the
world. Individuals are seduced into this because those
giving away or selling their Compass readings seem
very successful. The look of *success* sells Compass
readings. Now I'm not talking about shyster or rip-off
people. I'm talking about the run-of-the-mill, ordinary

individual that thinks someone else can career like they did and get similar results. Nor am I suggesting that one can't receive help and inspiration from such interaction. But, I am suggesting that when you get intimately involved with your Career Compass information, you'll find that someone else's information is interesting but not very useful. Until that time, you're living with the illusion that someone else knows more than you do. Finding your way is dependent on valuing and using your own Career Compass readings.

Quantum physics gave us a quantum leap in specifically suggesting that we create our own reality, so it gave us permission to own our reality, to own our myth, to rely on it, to love it, because that's the way things are. Finding your way is highly dependent on letting go of someone else's Career Compass readings which contain only their mythology. Start to read your own Career Compass and trust your own myth so you can get on with the business of doing what you came to earth to do which is unique and individual. Life now is giving us the opportunity to abandon others' directives and honor our own. But, most of us have tended to think that mythologies were only linked to literature, not to everyday living.

Personal Mythologies

Each of us has our own mythologies. "A myth is a living thing and exists within every person," says Robert A. Johnson in his book *HE: Understanding Masculine Psychology.* And no one myth is any better than another. But, one myth can exert more power than another. This can be seen in the myths being used to guide our nation's nuclear defense policies today. Some federal officials would rather we believe *their* mythologies about nuclear war than our own. They go so far as to call what some of us believe a *myth* and what *they* believe the *truth*.

An article about nuclear holocaust in the *Los Angeles Times* cited two such myths: (1) that the strategy of mutual nuclear deterrence is unsafe and unworkable; and (2) that those in government who conceived this strategy of deterrence are insensitive to the real dangers of nuclear war. It attributes these myths in part to the fact that "the political leaders and military theorists are cut off from reality and only understand their own Strangelovian concepts." The article suggests that "if we're to have an informed debate on the nuclear problem, it's important to understand the realities that these myths obscure."

Yet, the new physics tells us there's no such thing as objectivity, we can't remove ourselves from the picture. The human mind can't explore reality; it can only explore ideas about reality. Therefore, what each side is talking about is only its *ideas* about reality— and *not what really is.* One idea can't be a myth and the other a reality. Both are myths.

Finding Your Way: Going with the Flow

In finding your way, it's important to cooperate with life. Cooperating with life means *going with the flow* which gives you the feeling of attunement and oneness. Cooperating with life means going with *your* flow, not someone else's. So, ask yourself—are you ready to listen to your own inner feelings and put them into action?

The fact is that most of us go with life's flow most of the time. It's difficult to do otherwise. While moving along in the stop-and-go traffic of life, quickly changing lanes, slamming on your brakes, or gunning into the rush can be disastrous. You have a responsibility to yourself and to others to stay in your lane of life until you decide what to do next. Then you signal your intentions. If you need to stop, for example, pull over onto the shoulder. If you don't do so carefully, you can wreck your life and many others.

This isn't to say that you must stay in the same boring lane or on the same crowded road or even go in the same routine direction any longer than you want to.

It's your choice when and how you change your pattern. The problem is that life's traffic jams sometimes slow us down. Roads under construction force us to take maddening detours. Dead ends frustrate and confuse us. We get lost. The traffic of life moves and changes continually, just as the universe does. We have no choice but to accept and deal with it.

Yet, if most of us go with life's flow most of the time, how can we make personal choices? The trick is to go with the flow that feels *right* to you at the *moment*. Live in the *now*. If you need to move in a new direction that you sense is important to you, give a clear signal and head off in that new direction. Follow your Career Compass.

For instance, George Marciano invested $150,000 in manufacturing stone-washed denims at a time when designer jeans had faded from fashion. Our nation's economy was at an all-time low. Buyers who first saw his new look laughed him right out of their offices. They said the jeans were too tight and too sexy and looked like they'd been used. One year later, however, Marciano had grossed $15 million from the sales of his stone-washed jeans. He had faith in the rhythms of his life and of the marketplace. He trusted what he knew, and it worked for him.

Following Your Career Compass

As you follow your Career Compass—your experience, intelligence, and intuition—there may be times when your life activities don't seem to make much sense to you. As long as you feel that what you're doing is right—that's what's important. Your feelings and your actions may even surprise you at times. Sometimes, they may not feel quite right, but you know that what's happening is inevitable.

When you meet inevitable roadblocks, don't use energy trying to hurdle them. In life, two negatives don't make a positive. They make anger and frustration. They debilitate and disarm you. Better to find an open road and move forward. As we've seen, a change in your life can set you free, but only if you know to head for freedom. This sometimes means experiencing a *little death*.

Set

Experiencing Little Deaths

Stanley Keleman, in his book *Living Your Dying,* talks about death on two levels: big dying and little dying. Big dying is our physical death. Little dying is what we experience when we break old relationships, old ways of doing, being, thinking, and the like.

In finding our way, it's necessary to recognize and welcome the little deaths we experience in our daily living. The other side of little deaths is little births. Just as we experience turning points in society, we also experience them in our individual lives. Becoming aware of our turning points and how to handle them is the way we learn about our own transformations. We learn how to lose *old boundaries* and how to form *new boundaries*.

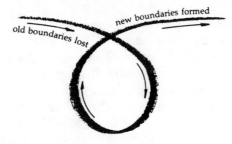

old boundaries lost   new boundaries formed

Used with permission

In losing or transcending old boundaries, we experience feelings akin to the dying and death stages described by pioneering researcher Dr. Elisabeth Kubler-Ross in her book *On Death and Dying*. This is illustrated by Fran Cey's account of the sudden change in the *work career* of her husband, baseball player Ron Cey.

After many years with the Los Angeles Dodgers, third baseman Ron Cey was traded to the Chicago Cubs. His wife, Fran, describes Ron's feelings of the inevitability of the trade:

> This would have been his 10th year with the Dodgers, and he thought he'd finish out with them. But, the dominoes started to fall with Davey (Lopes, who was traded to Oakland), and then Garvey (Steve, who went to San Diego). You could see what was coming. Through the last year, Ron has gone through Kubler-Ross' death and dying stages.

> First, the anger, then the denial. Then the 'Why me?' All that took a year. Now he's not only accepting it (being traded), he's elated. After a year of pain, when they asked him to waiver (Cey had a no-cut contract with the Dodgers), the decision took him two minutes.

Dying, death, and rebirth are inevitable parts of the rhythm of the universe. They are all possible results of change. We grow and strengthen and/or we die. So it is in nature. Some insects live for their assigned life span of one day and then die. Some trees live for centuries and then die. So it is also with suns and solar systems and galaxies. And with relationships and jobs—they grow or they die. It's the natural course of all things and events in the universe to end their appointed terms.

Little Deaths: Leaving a Job

Another example of a turning point was that experienced by the California college professor who, with his colleague had won an award as outstanding teacher. On receiving the award, his colleague vowed she'd "spend the rest of her life living up to it." Hearing her words, the professor thought to himself, "You've got to be kidding." His reaction was based on his experience. The stress of teaching and of battling an ever-dwindling budget and the general lack of appreciation for teachers had all affected his health. Two months earlier, he had been rushed to a hospital for an emergency ileostomy and colectomy. He said at the time, "I've given them my colon. I don't intend to give them anything else."

Go

A Different Reading of the Career Compass

Recognizing our own mythology and going with our own flow, we all experience our "little deaths." We each get a different reading on our Career Compass.

Maybe you've read about the ex-veteran who served with America's armed forces in the Vietnam War. Since the end of that action, he's slipped back into Vietnam and Cambodia several times. His mission there is to search for American prisoners of war missing in action and never accounted for. It can be dangerous, expensive work. But, he believes in it, whether or not others do. It's important to him, and that's all that matters. His *Life* is career.

Remember our earlier discussion about dissipative structures—atoms, nature, the universe? It is dissipative structures, such as we humans, that make order out of seeming randomness and chaos. Our

lives are much like the patterns seen in a kaleidoscope. They continually fall into new, different
shapes and designs as we change our positions.

Finding Your Way: Direction Is a Matter of How You View It

Epictetus, a philosopher, in a field manual for
Roman soldiers said, "People are not disturbed by
things, but by the view they take of things" (Higginson,
1955). Having or not having direction, then, is determined by how you view it. At times you may think
you don't have direction. What may be the case, however, is that your work career needs more focus. Your
life *does* have direction, whether you recognize it or
not. You get up in the morning, get dressed, and go
about your chores. You move through the day with
direction. What you may mean by *having no direction* is that part of your life doesn't feel right. Something isn't working. Like a clouded lens, you're out of
focus.

Feeling out of focus on one part of your life is
different from having no overall direction. However,
if you direct considerable energy to *feeling* directionless, it becomes more difficult to recognize a direction.
What we focus on often manifests. We get what we
think. Jane Roberts, in her book *The Individual and
the Nature of Mass Events*, suggests we are hypno-
tized into believing that our feelings arise *in response*
to events. Roberts, however, notes that our feelings
cause the events we perceive. Then we react to those
events. A psychological law is at work here: images or
mental pictures and ideas tend to produce the physical conditions and the external acts that correspond to
them.

The Good News about Being Directionless

Earlier we saw that order grows out of chaos (dissipative structures). So does direction in life. If you don't occasionally feel directionless, you won't fully appreciate having a feeling of direction and purpose. Most of us don't truly appreciate and enjoy having something until we don't have it. (And then, some of us even find we don't really want it after all.) So the next time you feel as though you're drifting aimlessly and without direction, allow yourself to experience it, feel it, learn from it. Know that feeling directionless can spur you into action. Such action can help you to become clearer.

Sometimes feeling directionless has an opposite effect—depression, because you don't think you're making the grade. This is where your *judge* goes to work and you begin to do negative affirmations. You say such things as "I'm not going anywhere," or "What happened to me? Here I am 30 years old, with a college degree, and I hate my work." You continue to tell yourself how much you don't have, and soon you start to believe it. You have programmed yourself.

Life is like a manuscript that you keep writing and revising.

Finding Your Way: Explore

One of the best ways to gain work-career direction is to explore possibilities. Talk with people you think can help you—particularly those who will encourage you to be *you*. Find out, by talking with them, what you need to know. This statement sounds easy. But, too often in life, we don't even know what we don't know. Entire work careers that you've never imagined may await you. You may be able to work or start your own business in areas you never considered—maybe you didn't even know they exist. Remember, we choose what we know.

An optometrist told me that his son had wanted to be an optometrist until he spent a summer in California. There, he went scuba diving for the first time and grew interested in deep-sea life. In time, he decided to become a marine biologist. As he experiences life, his work preferences will continue to change. That is *Life*-as-career.

The first step, then, is to explore. Date and record the information in a spiral notebook so it'll be handy for review. When you explore, you find. Finding can be enlightening. Enlightenment is knowing. Knowing builds confidence. Confidence is you living *Life*-as-career. Follow this path, and you'll gather a fund of new ideas. Not from the books nor from the teachings of others, but from and by yourself. After all, life is a manuscript that you keep writing and revising. That's what *Life*-as-career is all about.

Experience is your best teacher and wisest counselor. As Walt Whitman writes in *Leaves of Grass*:

> You shall no longer take things at second or third hand...nor look through the eyes of the dead...nor feed on the spectres in books. You shall not look through my eyes either, nor take things from me. You shall listen to all sides and filter them for yourself.

Finding Your Way: Right Is What Remains after We've Gone (We Think) Wrong

While we may not do as well as we want to, we must be careful how we describe things to ourselves because it determines how we feel about them. If we tell ourselves we're failures, then we send negative feelings into our bodies. If we say, we have fallen short, but we're halfway there, we give our bodies positive feelings. By sending positive signals to our bodies, we improve our physical health.

The next step is to continue to take yourself and life as they come. Some things work. Some don't. And some things work better than others. As you follow this trial and error process, your accuracy will improve. You'll set better objectives—and reach more of them. Meanwhile, try not to make too much of your misses and not enough of your hits. Find a balance between them. And don't punish yourself with phrases like, "If only I had..." or "What I should have done is...."

Instead, adopt Buckminster Fuller's philosophy: when you make a decision that doesn't work (that some people call wrong), you're closer to the truth than when you started. Even Thomas Edison seemed to support this view. On one occasion, Edison was showing some distinguished visitors through his Menlo Park laboratory. He proudly pointed out experiment after experiment—hundreds of them.

"Are these your successes?" one visitor asked.

"No," Edison smiled. "These are my failures." By 1879, Edison had racked up the sizeable sum of $40,000 in failures while trying to develop a working filament for his new incandescent lamp. Fortunately, for us all, Edison didn't grow discouraged and give up. Instead, he pressed on and at last found the ideal filament: carbonized bamboo. What is now known as the electric light was officially invented in 1879—the glowing result of all Edison's previous failures.

Finding Your Way:
Those Empty-Space Days

Empty-Space Days: When All Is Forgotten

As you're finding your way, remember that life

does have empty-space days. Often on such days, our memory is less than reliable. We tend to forget our past achievements and think that we're lost—and will continue to be. We also tend to think on these days that we haven't succeeded at anything in life. One good remedy for these empty-space days is to review our past achievements. It'll help you to remember who you are—and what you've done.

Other good remedies are:

- clean/organize your closets and drawers;
- catch up on sleep, review your diet;
- shop, work on hobbies;
- listen to good music, play golf;
- clean out the garage;
- tune your body (visit a gym or spa), jog;
- wash the car; work in the garden; or
- just "putter" around.

Learn to appreciate your empty-space days. They're given to you to relax and refresh you and to enable you to learn more about yourself.

Angels fly because they take themselves lightly.

Carol describes her empty-space days as times of *rejuvenation*. She's content to just putter around, cleaning closets, organizing her kitchen, planting bulbs in the garden, or whatever else occurs to her. Sometimes she goes shopping, but she seldom buys anything because she's found that later she usually doesn't like what she buys on empty-space times. Carol knows such days aren't wasted. They're full, but different. She readily admits she doesn't want them to come one after another. But, she's learned to see them as days of reflection. So she no longer judges them. In fact, she finds that empty-space days help her to move more easily through the eye of the tornado of change that's now happening in her life!

Carol now believes that her empty-space days contribute to her own personal understanding of what it is like being fully human. Many of us are now awakening to this possibility.

Try Again

Ready, Set...

Part of the problem in finding your way is *readiness*. We all have opinions about who should be ready for what and when. For example, if you're not ready to move forward, professionals are apt to suggest you're *behind*, a career underachiever. We measure and judge people using our own standards and our own misperceptions of what *is* and what *should be*.

Discussing the "underachiever-overachiever," noted linguist Neil Postman asks, "Does the under-achiever mean a person with a whole lot of smart who's doing poorly? Is an overachiever a person with a whole lot of dumb who does good?"

Today, a great many people believe they're career underachievers. And they feel guilty about it. So they try to play catch-up. To make matters worse, many of us are guilty of causing *others* to feel *behind* in life or in work career. Young people experience this pressure to achieve early. For example, "You must decide what you want to do with your life by Monday morning. That's when class scheduling starts." Or, "If you don't take college preparatory subjects starting in the eighth grade, you'll have a hard time getting into college. Then you'll wish you had." And on and on. The achiever tradition programs and pressures us, even when we enter the job market. "If you don't make it by 30, you're finished."

This emphasis on achievement may continue to

dog us all our lives. What's called a *mid-life crisis* might happen because, at 40 or 50, we find we're not yet running IBM or General Motors. And we're not doing as well as some of our friends. So, we think we've failed. Society tells us so. After all, society warned us about underachieving when we were age 7, and sure enough, we tell ourselves we *are*. "It's too late now. I haven't 'done it' and I never will now. I've spent all my adult life working in this place, instead of getting to the top, and now I think that I'll panic and start to scream..." And another dropout from the employment mainstream is born. This dropout was conceived and assured back in grade school, when he started being told, "You should," "You'd better," and "If you don't..."

Finding Your Way:
Going with Life's Rhythms

Each of us grows and develops according to our own time clock. We, and only we, know when we're ready to do something. We simply need to quiet ourselves and listen to the rhythms of our bodies, minds, and souls. Children do it. But, society programs out of us much of this wonderful early sense of being in-touch-with-self. Many of us even become afraid to listen to our own inner messages. Often, they're quite different from what we're doing externally. Each of us is a unique rhythm in universe. When we begin at last to move to our special rhythm, we feel whole.

The presence and specialness of our own personal rhythms are noted even in the early scriptures. For example, Ecclesiastes 3:1 declares:

> To everything there is a season, and a
> time to every purpose under the heaven.

And the rhythms of the universe—and of each of us—are cited in the *Tao,* as well:

The Universe is sacred.
You cannot improve it.
If you try to change it, you will ruin it.
If you try to hold it, you will lose it.
So, sometimes things are ahead and some-
     times they are behind.
Sometimes breathing is hard, sometimes
     it comes easily.
Sometimes there is strength and sometimes
     weakness;
Sometimes one is up and sometimes down.

Fritjof Capra, author of *The Turning Point,* suggests:

In the future elaboration of the new
world view, the notion of rhythm is likely
to play a fundamental role... Rhythmic
patterns seem to be manifest at all levels.
Atoms are patterns of probability waves,
molecules, and vibrating structures, and
organisms are multidimensional,
interdependent patterns of fluctuations.
Plants, animals, and human beings
undergo cycles of activity and rest.

Just as we all experience cycles of activity and
rest, so we are all part of the vibrating rhythms of the
universe. These rhythmic patterns and frequencies,
infinite in number, are a universal phenomenon,
universal laws beyond breaking. Their vibrations
may change in frequency but not in their presence.
     Life, then, is rhythm and subject to immutable
universal law. *Life*-as-career is life in rhythm.

JoAnn's Rhythm

After two years of college, JoAnn dropped out of
school, got married, had five children, and never re-

turned to school, never held a job. However, she continued to read, learn, and stay interested in herself. Now that her children are grown, JoAnn has decided to become a free-lance writer. She loves the challenge of it and feels that it's right for her. She says that if she had her life to live over, given the same circumstances, she wouldn't change much. Everything came for her in its own time. And she never lost the vision. She believed in herself. Her life pleases her. And that's what matters, isn't it?

Like JoAnn, all of us live according to our own rhythms and vibrations.

Another Rhythm: New Breed of Hobos Riding the Rails

Also following their own life rhythms is today's new breed of hobos. Many of them come from smoke-stack-industry states in the Northeast, where they lost their jobs. Railriding is observed today at freight yards nationwide. At the Colton, California station, a major switching yard for both the Sante Fe and Southern Pacific Railroads, it's estimated that the number of transient men riding the rails has doubled in recent years. As many as 40 a day pass through. Whether any of them has found glory that rail-riding Woody Guthrie was searching for when he passed this way in the 1930s isn't known.

More and more of these men riding the rails are younger. And some transients are women—and children, even whole families. Rhythms of this sort transport not only the body, but the mind and soul. It takes a real feeling of belief that there's something *out there* to prompt a man, woman, or family to swing onto a freight train to follow it.

Each of these railriders moves to a different, personal rhythm. Just as, currently, nearly 5 billion persons worldwide are moving to billions of different rhythms and realities.

The Rhythm of Roving Airline Employees

Still other rhythms fill the lives of the nation's roving bands of airline employees who work in one place and live in another. This lifestyle, earlier reserved for pilots and flight attendants, is now being shared by ground employees as well. One man works in Torrance, California and tries to spend his days off with his wife and daughter in Butler, New Jersey. He's one of a growing number of airline employees who live out of suitcases and eat in cafes during the week. These Gypsy workers are victims of industry cutbacks.

Airline pilots are also being dislocated, for the same reason. According to the Airline Pilots' Association, 25 percent of its 33,000 members "have suffered some sort of dislocation" because of deregulation and cutbacks. At Los Angeles International Airport alone, some 300 airline employees commute from homes in other parts of the country. If you earn enough, you can do it.

One airline pilot lives on a large farm in central Missouri. When it's time to fly, he jumps in his private plane, takes off from his own strip, flies to Kansas City, parks his plane, and climbs aboard the company airliner. That's rhythm with style.

Each of us, then, lives and moves to our individual rhythms. And we can only hear and move to our own rhythms—no one else's.

If you don't know where you're going, any path will do.
        Brian Anderson

As you make your way in *Life*-as-career, you become more aware of the beating, pulsating rhythms of the universe. You start to feel them, to understand them. You begin to respond and move to their gentle pull. If your life is filled with too much noise and confusion—if there's too much static—you may not hear them. Life's rhythms won't shout at you and clamor for attention. They are subtle, persistent forces. They also have curious methods of reaching you. If you don't—or won't—listen, they find ways to get your attention: headaches are one, ulcers another. You probably can recall still other attention-getting signals of your own.

As you hear and feel life's rhythms, you begin to accept them. You not only experience change, you welcome it. You continue to live your life, yet you flow with the rhythms of the universe. You move from this point to that to the other. Sometimes you feel surprised, sometimes angry, sometimes frustrated. But you become more and more aware that the ebb and flow of life is inevitable, eternal. With its movement, you grow. You even bend when you must, stand strong when you must. And you feel the joy of the newness that is each moment of life each day. You understand that you are in tune with the forces of the universe. You're also aware of yourself in the *now*. All that comes to you and through you— all your previous *nows*—serve to further the *whole* that is the wonderful and unique *you*.

8

LIFE-AS-CAREER: A WORK OF YOUR OWN—FULLERING

Differences

Traditional career focuses on getting a job, while Lifecareer expands livelihood to include **both** getting a job **and** creating a work of one's own.

Each of us needs a work of our own. Something we love to do. Something that gives us joy. Jim Haynes calls this "fullering." In his book *Workers of the World Unite and Stop Working,* he describes the joy and freedom that fullering has brought to his own life:

> At the moment I am involved in a number of projects. I never think of them as jobs or as 'my work.' I teach at the University of Paris. I am trying to write several books and a movie script. I help administrate a small publishing and printing company... From time to time I pro-

duce magazine and newspaper articles
and involve myself with other crazy and
delightful projects. Only the university
provides a regular source of income. Yet,
I would gladly teach without payment.
And...if I had plenty of money, I would
pay for the right to teach. It, too, is fullering! None of these activities can be
classified as work for me. There are no
clocks to punch, no overtime payments,
no union, no pressures, no pain. I enjoy
them all.

Jim Haynes thrives on having a work of his own.
Let's take a closer look at fullering—and how it can
enhance *your* life, as well.

The Joys of Fullering

"Fullering" means joyful energy-spending, not
work-drudgery. When you truly enjoy what you do,
you're *fuller*—that is, happier and more fulfilled.

Simply explained, if you don't like what you do
(whether you work for yourself or another), that's
work. If you love what you do, that's *fullering*. In this
chapter, you'll learn more about how to:

- *fuller* (do what you love, for yourself or another);
- rely on and be guided by your experience, intelligence, and intuition;
- trust that life *does* know what it's doing.

To do what you love full-time, you must have
your survival needs met, such as your needs for food
and shelter. You must also have a sense of belonging.

Fullering, in Buckminster Fuller's view, looks at
meeting survival needs this way: when you use energy joyfully and in harmony with life, working for
the good of all people, your survival needs are less

difficult to meet. Why? Because you're doing what you care about for the good of all. As John Braine once observed:

> ...on the whole, people who enjoy their jobs make more money than those who don't, for the simple reason that they do their jobs better. They do their jobs better because they're not primarily interested in the money. That's the Catch 22 of work.

For 53 years, Buckminster Fuller devoted his creative energy to pursuing his own work and had abiding faith that his survival needs would be met. This is echoed in the words he inscribed in my copy of his book, *Critical Path*: "To Anna, With faith in the comprehensive, incisive intellectual integrity manifest by the universe." Fuller had faith that *life* really *does* know what it's doing. He also knew that life works. One reason it works is that people didn't invent it and can't *improve upon it*. But, they *can* use it.

Nowhere to Go But Up

Today, millions of people throughout the United States have nowhere to go but up. These persons include the unemployed and those subsisting below the poverty level. Since they've little to lose, they could experiment with *fullering*—doing something they love while trusting *life*. Who are these people? Recently, they assumed the following numbers:

- •32 million people were unemployed, 27 to 49 weeks;
- •14 million preferred to work full-time but had to work part-time;
- •4 million working full-time had earnings below the minimum wage equivalent of $6,700 per year. (U. S. Dept of Labor, 1987)

It appears that over 30 million people throughout
the United States could use a new strategy. Added to
this are those who need more challenge and creativity in their lives.

Is It Possible for These People to *Fuller*?

It's not only possible, it's beginning to happen. As
people like these experience the good feeling of having a work of their own and realize they can *do* it,
they're wanting to do more and more.

For example, there's Sally, who lives in Appala-
chia. She's a high school graduate who couldn't find
work. So she created her own work, doing something
she loves to do. Sally started a service that recruits
and supplies workers to do odd jobs—from light
hauling and home repair to running errands for shut-
ins. She follows up on the placements—makes certain
the workers show up and do well—and she charges
for the service.

One day recently, Sally had 30 people working.
She charges a one-time finder's fee of $5.00 for each
placement. So, in a single day, she earned $150. It
took many phone calls—it's a lot of work—but Sally
enjoys it. She's learning from it. Chances are she'll go
on to turn it into a first-class placement service. And
she's never read a book or attended a seminar on how
to do it. She simply used her experience, her intelligence, and her intuition. She figured it out for herself.

No, Sally wasn't the valedictorian of her class. In
fact, she just barely made it through high school. And
she's never heard of *fullering*. But, she's *fullering*
naturally. When she was shut out of the work force,
Sally didn't despair. She simply started to do what
seemed right at the moment—and felt good about it.
She turned what seemed a crisis into an *opportunity*.

How Do You Know If You're Fullering?

That warm, happy feeling you get when you're doing something you love can be a powerful motivator. The happier you get, the more you want, and that's how *fullering* works. It's like love: it feels wonderful. Barbara Marx Hubbard (*Keynote at the Assembly to Advance Career, University of Southern California,*) says it this way:

> The signal that you're doing the right thing isn't just pleasure or whimsical happiness, it's joy. And I call it the 'Compass of Joy.' That has been my compass through my whole life. It's when I have felt pain, I've said, 'thank you, that's not the way you're meant to go.' And I use it as a very deep lesson... Pain is always teaching you something. And then, you move like a little beam of light.

> Teilhard de Chardin, a religious philosopher, called it 'tatoney,' tapping like a blind person in the dark with a white cane. You tap, tap, tap, tap until you get a shot of joy. 'Aha, go that way a little bit more. Aha, go that way.' And if you'll do that, and you can trust your feelings enough to do it, you'll find your way. It's a really fascinating choice process going on here, because we're moving from outer direction to inner direction.

Hubbard goes on to discuss a Stanford Research Institute study of the values and lifestyles of Americans. This study found that some 25 million Americans are now moving from outer-directed to inner-directed value systems. In an outer-directed value system, you take your lead from somebody else, who tells you how it is for you and everybody else. An inner-directed value system is one that comes from deep within you.

Hubbard noted that our need to have someone else tell us what to do "...is crumbling. We're turning within, being directed and guided by our own inner knowing. The way we know if we're following our inner wisdom is by the deep inner experience of joy." This sometimes calls for us to live with ambiguity and uncertainty. We who are *fullering* know ambiguity and uncertainty well. We also know that *life does know what it's doing*.

A colleague, who works holistically, told a client, who had tried all the traditional approaches, to use the *Lifecareer* and *fullering* approaches instead. She was told "Decide what you want in your life and work-career, then jot it down. Be honest about your wants and needs, and write from the heart. Also note ways to get your wants and needs." The client reported that this exercise had changed her life—for the better. She said:

> What you told me works. You asked me
> to write down what I was looking for.
> You told me to be open and it'd come to
> me. I then began to consider and visual-
> ize long-term intentions, what I wanted,
> leaving the 'how' to *life*. I wanted to live
> my philosophy being who I was and
> make money, too. But, it wasn't easy
> with my subconscious level saying, "You
> can't do that, it's not possible." But, when
> I committed to it with full faith, my
> subconscious believed it, and away I

went. What you say works. It's kind of
spooky.

I then bought a journal and carried it
with me. When I think of an idea, I write
it down. Einstein said your mind should
be where you work things out, not store
a bunch of stuff. So I use my mind for
working things out and I organize it to
find what I need.

Living *Life*-as-career and fullering, I'm
becoming the person I want to be. It's not
the goal but the journey that's important.

The above may sound too simplistic and for
some people it may not work quite so quickly;
whereas for others it may not work at all. But for
this client it did work and made all the difference in
her life. I continue to be impressed by what changes
a life. Sometimes it's just a word, a phrase, or the
right structure at the right time. *Right* being defined
as what the individual construes as *right*.

Two Approaches to Earning a Living

The Be-Do-Have Approach

Shakti Gawain in her book, *Creative Visualization*, discusses the two basic approaches to earning a
living:
    The first, from who you are (fullering), and the
second from how much money you can make
(working).
    Here are the basic steps of the *who you are*
(fullering) approach which also can be called the Be-
Do-Have approach:

(1) You start with *who you are*;

(2) Find activities that harmonize with
   who you are;

(3) In order to have whatever it is
   you're wanting.

This means you must "...first *be* who you are, then *do* what you need to do, to *have* what you want." Today, more and more of us, including many young people, are learning *to fuller*, to do what we love and what we feel good doing. We're also learning that it's healthy, both physically and psychologically. And many people are making a great deal of money at it. The reason is simple: they enjoy what they do, so they do it well. They do it wholeheartedly. Additionally, many of them have good networks of social contacts and use them well. People like these usually have high positive-energy levels. And they aren't apt to complain or find fault with the world around them. They're too busy living Life-as-career.

In contrast, some people do what they love and don't *make much money* at it, but they love their lifestyles. These people also have high positive-energy levels and are not complainers. They, too, are busy living Life-as-career.

The Have-Do-Be Approach

In contrast, the Have-Do-Be approach closely reflects our Western lifestyles today:

(1) Have more things or money;

(2) To do more...;

(3) In order to be *happier*.

Most Americans still follow this approach, though their numbers are dwindling. You work at a job to have the money for things: cars, houses, stereos, vacation cruises, and the like. When you work primarily to support material things, whether you're self-employed or work for someone else, it's more difficult to change direction quickly because you're tied to your things and your need for money to pay for them. But, when your life purpose is primary and your material needs secondary, then it's easier to go for what you care about. For example, to change jobs, to start your own business, to travel or to move. Many people hate what they do, but feel they're *locked in* by the need to finance their material things. So they forego their dreams and wishes, sometimes permanently.

Everything has its cost — working for someone else and fullering. Sometimes the cost is hidden. Somtimes we pay more than we expect, sometimes we find a bargain. Cost is not punishment, but the way Life is.

Why Should I Seriously Consider Fullering?

Today's New Work-Career Pattern: Piecing Together Income

Earning income from a variety of activities—instead of from just one job—is fast becoming the new work-career pattern in the United States. How many people do you know who are already earning money from more than one source, including interest and other investment income? We recently had a visit from a friend who's doing this. He gets income from his work as a consultant, teacher, salesperson, newsletter editor, and developer of computer programs. "I'm less sure of my monthly income," he said, "but I'm more sure of my intellectual stimulation and my need to be on my toes and use my intelligence. It's interesting how this all started. One day, I just got to the point where I was willing to forego a secure weekly paycheck to acknowledge my need to grow, and do more different and challenging activities." However, he admits he has his down days, but as he says, "Sure, I have my down days, but I had those when I worked for someone else. The bonus I now have is that I love what I'm doing. As a result, I feel better physically and mentally—my body is getting the joy message."

When we work for ourselves, we unleash our intelligence and creativity. As we apply them freely, we produce wonderful, surprising things—some that generate income for us. We also make mistakes rapidly, so we can learn more quickly. But, to do all this, we first must move from *either/or* thinking to *both/and* thinking.

Either/Or Thinking Still Prevails

The notion that one *either* has a job *or* is self-employed has long prevailed—and still does today. Though factory jobs are steadily dwindling in number and other types of jobs are rapidly being replaced by automation, traditional *get a job* thinking continues to dominate. The reason? Many people have difficulty expanding their thinking to include the choice of making work for themselves.

Today, a fair number of young people are beginning to understand that they may have to *make* their jobs. Some are beginning to enroll, in large numbers, in college and university entrepreneur programs across the nation. In these programs, they learn how to conceive, launch, and operate their own businesses. On the other hand, some enterprising high school students are learning how to do this by *doing* it.

Mike was one of those students. At 15, he got a job at a restaurant in his home town selling "sandwiches and ice cream and stuff like that." The restaurant contained two tables and six chairs. Mike worked there for about a year and saved part of his $2.50 an hour earnings. One day, he came to work and saw that the restaurant was for sale. He checked into it. The owner contacted Mike's father, and Mike soon bought the restaurant for about $10,000, with bank loans and help from his grandmother. At age 16, Mike owned his own business. Mike says that owning the restaurant could have hurt his grades, instead his grades came up. After graduating from high school, Mike sold the restaurant and, in April 1983, bought and paid cash for a grocery store which he still owns.

Mike learned how to be a business owner by *being* one. He also learned that *fullering* increased his confidence and prepared him for even greater challenges.

Both/And Is Gaining Popularity— by Necessity

Having *both* a business on the side *and* a part- or full-time job working for someone else may help many to survive today's growing unemployment, underemployment, and re-employment problems. For some, income from their job will help cover the costs of launching a new business. Families and friends sometimes join forces to help one another get started.

For many reasons, home-front businesses are becoming both common and popular—by necessity. Alvin Toffler, in *The Third Wave,* calls them *cottage industries*. They can be a good way to earn extra money while you continue to work part- or full-time at a job or other venture. While *cottage industry* tends to seem a little restrictive in concept—namely, making small products or delivering services—a *home-front business*, (a business based at home or nearby) can grow and flourish as large as your imagination.

My grandfather often said, "If you have one foot in industry and the other on the land, you won't have to worry." Times have changed, however, and my suggestion is that you place your faith squarely in your experience, your intelligence, and your intuition. And, if you need to, use a job to help you get more of what you want.

For a growing number of Americans, home-based businesses are becoming full-time ventures. It all depends on how you feel about the idea, about yourself, and about the lifestyle that goes with it.

A woman whose husband left her with $2,000 in the bank and young children to support had a life-direction problem. Since her strongest skill was writing, she decided to produce a newsletter for and about the various boutiques in her city. Her newsletter venture soon proved quite successful. She didn't call it *fullering*, but that is what she was doing. Then she started knitting and selling scarves to these same boutiques. The demand soon became so great that she had to buy a knitting machine and hire people to work for her. The business continued to grow, and she soon started to commercially manufacture knit scarves.

This woman didn't plan to become a manufacturer or to make a million dollars. She started by doing something she enjoyed; something she knew she could do without further training. Her success shows that, inch by inch, life's a cinch. As jobs grow more and more scarce, many of us will have to tap our intelligence and intuition in a similar way.

More and more individuals are starting to *fuller*, and advanced thinking companies are now encouraging their employees *to fuller*. They call it *Intrepreneurship*. That is, they encourage an employee to work on an idea that interests him or her, present it to the management, and if it's accepted, the employee is given financial backing and the support to get the idea going. If the product makes money, the employee gets a percentage of the profits. This is the company's way of keeping good employees around and interested, and business stimulated.

Further Advantages of Fullering

Another advantage of *fullering* is that it's flexible. You can start and stop it when you choose to. You're not locked in.

Take Mildred and Joe, for example. Mildred loved to bake whole-grain breads and muffins. She was constantly developing new, more delicious varieties, to the delight of her family and friends. Joe, her husband, enjoyed helping her. They decided to rent a small store on a well-traveled boulevard and market her baked goods from there. Soon, they had developed a fair number of regular customers. Then, Joe thought about packaging and selling the breads and muffins to a few local independent supermarkets. When the market managers proved receptive, Joe bought a small used panel truck and began delivering the orders to the markets before going to work each day. In time, he left his mundane job as a machinist to join Mildred in the business. In two years, their net income from the sale of baked goods has grown to $950 a week. How long will they continue their baking business? As long as they find it interesting and enjoyable.

Still other people *fuller* out of necessity. A recent Ph.D. graduate, for example, couldn't find a job. So she decided to piece together her income from several different pursuits. She presently consults on three projects for the State Department of Education. She teaches a night course in adolescent psychology. And she manages conferences for special groups twice a year.

Today, more and more people are turning to fullering. John, for example, didn't finish high school, but has worked as a plumber trainee for several years and enjoys it. Recently, John decided to start his own plumbing business. He passed the state exam and got a plumbing contractor's license. Then he ordered business cards and inserted a running ad in the local paper and in the Yellow Pages. Because John is honest, fair, and dependable, he now gets more work than he can handle.

This is the law of being — dharma: to do the work to which you are driven by your capacity and inner compulsion, rather than seeking to gain great success along a channel that is basically not yours.

Bhagavad Gita

Then there's Debby, who wrote a book-length manuscript and submitted it to publishers. She received fourteen rejections. At last, she decided to publish the work herself. She arranged to have it reviewed in several magazines and newspapers, secured a distribution firm to market it to bookstores, and sold copies of the book herself. Because of the favorable reviews the book received, Debby soon was approached by several publishers. By that time, she had grown weary of the marketing chores, so she gave it to a publisher—with good results. Debby is now writing another book. Also, she buys houses, refurbishes them, and sells them. Both pursuits have proven profitable for her. But, Debby knows that, in piecing together income, you need to have a variety of potential sources. So she's now considering signing up with a local speakers' bureau. If she does, she can add to her income by talking about her book at local conventions and conferences. Some appearances bring as much as $1,200.

Take It Slow—Experiment While You're Working

Having a job enables you to try new business ideas while you're still working. It also provides you with income to meet your needs and to help launch your business when you're ready to. This brings to mind a friend who worked in an aircraft factory and made jewelry in his spare time. He became good at it and soon began to sell his jewelry to some of his female co-workers. One Friday, his earnings from the jewelry he had made and sold to the women in the office were twice his factory paycheck. That's when he decided to quit his job and devote himself to making jewelry full time. "In the beginning," he recalls, "I made some ugly pieces. But, even *they* sold. My business has continued to grow, and I've done well. But, the best part of it is that I *love* what I do." This man never took a design class, and his jewelry is so beautiful that it rivals some of the finest. Design training might even have inhibited his natural, artistic ability.

We all have abundant skills we can use to earn money. But, some of us simply don't consider the value of our hidden abilities. We're often inclined to *hide our light under a bushel*. And the presence of the computer opens even more possibilities for some of us to make it on our own. For example, Richard Walker in *PC Magazine* notes that the experts predict a billion dollar market for educational software. Educational software is just one of the products headed for a market boom; many others will follow. What new product or service are you capable of developing? Think about it—and let your ideas evolve and grow.

Don't Wait Until Someone Else Kicks Your Card Table

What do you want your life to be? This is the time to take some chances, to risk, to put yourself squarely on the line. If you don't, the company you work for may force that change upon you. And when that happens, it can be more scary. Don't wait until someone else kicks your card table with your life puzzle on it—leaving you to pick up the pieces and put your life back together again. The power to choose what you want in life is *yours,* if you act on it. As the popular song lyrics tell us, "You've got to know when to hold 'em, know when to fold 'em, know when to walk away, know when to run."

This isn't to say that all jobs soon will disappear. Some people will always be able to get a job. This has been true since the earliest times. When prehistoric man needed help in foraging for food, he hired someone to help bag an animal. Maybe he paid the person in food or services. But, it was work. And so it'll always be. However, growing numbers of people won't be assured of future jobs as we know them today. Our industrial-scientific society is changing so rapidly that the nature of work and the work force, can only change as well. The old employment alliance is quickly being replaced with the new working arrangements. I'll say more about that in Chapter 13.

But, I'm Employed— and Happy About It

"Hold on," you say, "I'm happy in my job. I don't need to create any work. I love what I'm doing." Maybe. But just because you're content now doesn't mean you will be next year. Even if nothing else changes, *you will change.* All of us do—every second, every minute. And the best time to think about change is when you're happy and content.

Even if you have a wonderful livelihood, an income source that fully supports you, remember change. It's coming your way. It's drawing closer and closer. Remember, that *every* system is a potential dissipative structure. That is, it can experience radical changes. Your job is no exception.

Today, many highly qualified people are walking the streets without work, wondering what happened. They include skilled technicians, professors, chemists, aeronautical engineers, steel workers, computer programmers, teachers, researchers, and management executives. And their numbers are growing. Most of them didn't expect or prepare for the change that cost them their jobs. But, you *can.*

Discover Your Troy

Noted writer Ray Bradbury tells the story of Heinrich Schliemann, who wanted to find the legendary city of Troy described in the writings of Homer. People kept telling Schliemann that Troy didn't really exist, that it was only a fictional place, like Atlantis. However, Schliemann refused to listen. Instead, he saved his money and, around 45 years of age, set out to find the city of Troy. He found not one, but *several* cities of Troy—all built upon one another. He continued to believe in and to follow his dream. In the end, many more Troys, at various levels of civilization and sophistication, were found. *That's* making a dream come true!

Each of us needs to search for our own Troy, though others around us think we'll never find it or that we don't have what it takes. We hear statements like, "People will never buy that," or "It's been done already," or even, "Why don't you get a job instead?" They all suggest that *you* don't know where Troy is, but that *they* do. To which you might respond, "If you're so smart, why aren't *you* rich?" Or "president?" Or even, "Then why haven't *you* found Troy?"

Deep within, you know where *your* Troy is. You know that it lies silently in your soul, waiting to be found. And you can find it if you choose to.

My hope is that this book will move you to start exploring. That's what this book is all about. It's meant to convey that your dreams are right there, within you, waiting to be found and followed. Only *you* can find them. And you *can* find them. Not making it on someone else's terms, and succeeding on your own, is a matter of growth, of coming to trust yourself, and of learning from all those ways you've tried to go.

Ray Bradbury, the science-fiction writer, is a wonderful example of this idea. His words describe the process eloquently.

The Growing Into Me

I will live
If I live at all
Not because anyone else,
For I wonder if they did,
But because I knew me,
Or tried to know
All the ways I tried to go,
Or when I went,
The messages I sent to me
And I received,
The notions I conceived and
wrote away
And saved
The fears I braved, the loves I won or lost,
The costing of it all, in blood and dreams,
My schemes to last forever
As a child,
The wildest proclamations that I gave
To save my soul and wits,
The judge that sits behind my eyes
And tries to weigh and know,
The growing into me
That was the boy that tried to be.
I have it all,
Oh, no, no, not put by in diary or note,

But tales I wrote
To dig me up and show my bones,
The loans I gave and took
From left hand to the right,
The nights I stayed up wrestling with death,
And stopped its breath;
Thus trapped in my machine,
And typed and bound,
I roped it round with gardened evergreen
And buried it in nouns and verbs
And gave it herbs to make it well,
A little while at least,
By reckoning it in poems,
Gave homes to dire doubts,
Put down so deep they never could return,
I yearned them forth with words
And charmed the doubting birds.
Well, that is it,
That was my life, that's what
I always hoped to be
Not knowing, known to others,
For they're blind, you see.
I will live
If I live at all
Because I tried,
And sometimes made it,
To know me.

Ray Bradbury - Collected Poems (1983)

9

THE TECHNOLOGY STORY: YOU DECIDE

Differences
In traditional career, social context is secondary;
in Lifecareer it is primary.

Robotics and Automation

As we discussed earlier, we each create our own reality; we decide what is real for us. Your belief system will signal what you think is real. Look at what you believe and you'll understand what reality you've created for yourself.

Regarding the effects of technology—robotics and automation—on the work force, at least two different realities have formed: one that thinks technology will create even more jobs than it eliminates; and a second that technology may not create a significant number of jobs. If the latter holds, then having a back-up plan would serve as a safety net. You, the reader, have to decide which of these realities feels right. If you choose the first reality, then you probably won't subscribe to the safety-net approach, however, you'll learn many livelihood lessons, so in that way, it may be a right turn for you. Choosing the second reality will give you a safety net, so if there's great prosperity in jobs, you'll be more than prepared. Besides, you'll have something to take care of your expanding creativity. Whichever approach you choose, it'll be right for the time of choice. So, let's look at the information.

By the year 2000, reports the U. S. Department of Commerce, half of our nation's adults will rely on home-based businesses for at least part of their income. Some 18 million people are already doing this. Many of them were forced to start their own businesses because they couldn't find jobs. Others choose to work from their homes because it feels right. As the increasing use of robotization in the United States sharply reduces jobs in business and industry, millions more may be forced to consider home-based businesses. However, it'll provide a golden opportunity to do something you love—to fuller and feel fuller. The trend has started as these figures show.

TABLE I
U. S. Robotics Industry

	1980	1981	1982	1983	1985	1990
Sales (Millions of $)	90	155	205	270	540	2070
Production	1450	2100	3075	4000	7715	31350

Source: *High Technology Industries: Profiles and Outlooks, The Robotics Industry.* U. S. Department of Commerce, International Trade Administration, April 1983.

As seen here, 2,100 robots were produced in 1981—a 44.8% increase over robots produced in 1980. By 1990, production could exceed 30,000 units. Add to this, the fact that in 1980, Japan produced 7,500 to 8,500 robots at a value of $660 million, has since produced thousands more, and is projected to produce an additional 52,000 to 56,000 robots at a value of $3.5 billion. These Japanese robots are now being marketed in the United States. Moreover, worldwide robotics development is now under way: in addition to Japan, West Germany, the United Kingdom, Sweden, Italy, Norway, and France are all producing robots.

What does all this mean? It means that the world robotics industry will continue to grow. And this growth will dramatically change job prospects for all of us. With machines doing most of the more repetitive and/or dangerous work and few technicians needed to maintain them, more and more people will be forced to look elsewhere for work or to consider starting a home business.

Today, businesses of every kind are becoming more automated, computerized, and robotized—for example, newspaper production plants. The Linotype machine which casts type one line at a time was used by many newspapers during much of this century. When it was introduced, it replaced the jobs of many people who set type manually or who used old typesetting devices. Still, the Linotype is a labor-intensive machine prone to frequent breakdowns. Even when semi-automatic Linotype machines were later developed that could be operated by lower-paid technicians, maintaining these machines was a major task. Then, low-maintenance, computer-driven typesetting machines were introduced. When they began to gain widespread acceptance in the newspaper industry in the 1970s, out went the jobs of thousands of well-paid Linotype operators and mechanics and of the lower-paid machine technicians as well.

The effect of microprocessors on office employment is difficult to predict. Analysts talk more about jobs *affected* instead of *eliminated*. But, the figures are dramatic.

The Robotization Effect

According to the 1988 U. S. Census data, approximately 33 million jobs in precision, production, operating, fabricating, and administrative support have the potential for robotization. As this happens, sizeable numbers of middle managers and administrators also may be displaced.

The findings of a Carnegie-Mellon University study suggest that 38 million of the nation's 50 million existing white-collar jobs eventually will be affected by automation. A vice president of strategic planning for Xerox Corporation offers the more conservative guess of 20 to 30 million jobs affected by 1990.

Meanwhile, in Western Europe, two British authors predict that nothing less than the collapse of work as a social institution will happen in the era of microprocessors. They suggest that it's impossible to overdramatize the expected crisis ahead because it threatens to strike a blow at the very core of the world's industrialized societies—the work ethic. Our social structure is based on this ethic, and now it appears that it may be rapidly dismantled along with the jobs of millions of workers.

On the other side of the coin, there are those who argue that technology and automation will provide even more jobs. Specifically, a recent study done by the National Academy of Sciences suggests that new industrial technologies do more to create jobs than they do to displace workers from obsolete jobs. The study suggests that "...throughout recent history, technological change has helped to increase the total number of people working and to raise their standards of living. We have every reason to believe this trend will continue" (Panel Says Automation, 1987b, p. 1).

But, look at the condition upon which the statement "throughout recent history" is based. It assumes we can know the future by examining the past. What is happening now has never happened before in human history. The capability of making machines and procedures obsolete within one or two years is a completely new phenomenon. So one cannot look at the future through the lens of the past as there are too many unknown factors.

Never before in human history have we had the technology to end most routine work — that one possibility will change all our futures significantly.

Further, the rate of unemployment and available jobs is a complex issue. Many things affect both simultaneously. Some of these factors are foreign competition, technological innovation other than automation, changes in consumer preferences, business bankruptcies, public policy and government spending, labor supply and skill demand.

However, a major dissipation is happening in the occupational structure which is changing work and work access for large numbers of people. Those who choose the safety-net approach and become aware of what may happen and then formulate a Plan B can reduce both psychological and physical stress, whereas those who believe that everything will be the same as earlier may find themselves in crisis. However one decides to think and believe about the occupational transformation now under way, there will be lessons to learn.

These are very exciting times in which to live as they provide genuine opportunity for growth, and the deliberate practice of Lifecareer.

But Won't the New Automated Machines Need People to Repair Them?

If you believe that when a machine replaces you on the job, you can get a position maintaining that machine, you may be in for a surprise. Robots, computers, and the like, work pretty well. Jobs repairing them don't abound. And probably won't. The reason? Take a look at the inner workings of your personal computer or of the models on display at your local computer store. You'll find they don't contain many parts that need repair.

Bob, for example, trained to become a robot technician. Now he complains that he can't find work. "The need for such technicians," he says, "was greatly exaggerated." So he's unemployed. You may be, too, if you stake your future on becoming a robot or computer technician.

This is a both/and universe. There's both free will and destiny. However we choose, the universe has all the bases covered.

Is Repetitive Work Disappearing?

The fear that automated machines will replace workers is valid and real since workers to date have done mostly jobs that machines can do. **Menial work as we know it is rapidly disappearing.** Job retraining isn't the solution when 30 million jobs disappear and over 104 million people need to earn a living. Instead, workers can be retrained to think *movement, change, and potential, not* stable and predictable. While we all experience change, still we expect things to stabilize. Many of us aren't yet convinced that both movement and change are here to stay. We keep hoping they'll go away or settle down somehow into an understandable pattern.

Shifting How We View Things

To help us shift our perception of this, **consider that the average length of time workers of all ages spend on one job in the United States is 4.2 years.** Viewed by age groups, the longest average time spent on one job is 12 years, and this is for workers in the 55 to 64 age group. Consider, too, **that 29 percent of the nation's workers stay on a job 1 year or less and that 13 percent stayed on a job from 6 to 9 years** (U. S. Department of Labor, 1987).

Also reflecting the rapid rate of change and mobility now under way is the average length of time a family or an individual occupies a purchased home in California. It's 5 years. Similarly, the time it takes to translate a scientific discovery into a marketable product has recently been reduced from 20 years to 5 years. And 5 years isn't much time to establish any type of pattern or stability as we know it. Our experience, then, is changing, and we're trying to stay abreast of it.

Change Is Being Felt at All Occupational Levels

High rates of displacements are expected to affect all areas of the nation's business—more bankruptcy petitions will be filed, more businesses will fail. This isn't coming, it's happening now. Old, established businesses are closing their doors. One, a large Los Angeles furniture store that had been in business for 104 years, recently was forced to shut down. And in 1983, 48 banks failed nationwide, marking the greatest number of bank failures in the United States since 1939, when 60 banks failed. But, in 1984, over 75 banks failed. And in 1986, 145 banks failed. This economic reconstruction is being felt by more and more people. Many of those who have lost their jobs, for example, are forced to forego their medical and dental needs. The result has been a drop in business for physicians and dentists, making them rethink their previous patterns. Some of them are re-examining their skills to determine what else they can do to supplement their incomes. More than a few physicians and dentists have started to write text-books. Others are writing novels. Still others are turning to a variety of income-producing pursuits. When technology cuts deep into any one occupation level, it affects all levels. So rethinking livelihood isn't confined to persons in any one occupational group, we'll all have to do it.

PART III

OVERCOMING OBSTACLES TO LIFECAREERING

10

DECISION MAKING: DOING WHAT COMES NATURALLY

Differences

In traditional career the focus is on right or wise decision making, whereas in Lifecareer it is on valuing both the right and left (what some call wrong) decisions.

In thinking about making a work of your own, how can you be *sure* you are making the right decision? You can't be. There are no right decisions, only decisions, and each one contributes to your learning. They all bring you closer to knowing what you want, what is right for you. That's why the decision-making process isn't spelled out for you in these pages. It doesn't need to be taught. In fact, while most of us make decisions regularly throughout our lives, we tend to do so rather willy-nilly. And the more we do, the more we learn about the process, and what is right for us.

You may argue that, when it comes to decision

making, some people don't seem to improve. But most of them would not agree. They like the way they make decisions. They believe they use intelligence to correct their experience and to make better choices. They just do so on *their* terms, not yours.

Making decisions is based on your perceptions of the world, your attitudes, your learning, your experience, your intuition. No one but *you* can make your decisions nor even teach you how to make them. All others can do is encourage you to listen to your inner voice—*really* listen—when decision time comes along. And that's every day.

Yes, we all can improve our decision-making skills. But, no, most of us don't want any help in making that improvement, thank you. We just want to continue practicing decision making knowing that if things don't go right they will go left, and therein will lie the learning.

The Snails

Even the snails that work the night shift in my patio are veteran decision-makers. They glide and slide past tasty plants that would certainly please their palates, to climb up onto a glass table and get at the young, tender plants there instead. They have even decided to liven up their menu with munches of collard, parsley, and sage. And this morning, I discovered they had started on the impatiens for dessert.

In intelligence, these single-minded creatures must rank in the bottom 10 percent of all life forms. Yet, they have needs, and they use their intelligence to fill these needs. They decide what to eat and what not to eat. Somehow, their tiny, mushy brains determine all they will do.

In their own instinctive, crawling, chewing ways, they fully live *Life*-as-career. The career of my snails, for example, appears to be leveling my herb garden. While this seems to me a perverse sort of life-work, to them it apparently makes perfect sense.

The Bacterium

Another example is the *Pseudomonal syringae* bacterium, which researchers say may be a cause of rain. Montana Agricultural Experiment Station researchers:

> ...stumbled on this novel theory when they were investigating how bacterial leaf blight, caused by the moisture-loving bacterium, gets around. They found *P. syringae* in clouds during the growing season and further discovered that it can cause ice crystals to form high in the air, a necessary precondition of rain. Plant pathologist David Sands theorizes that the organism, by causing rain, creates the right conditions on the ground for the bacterium to multiply, be picked up and carried aloft, cause more rain, and thus keep conditions to its liking for many miles around (Cox, p. 100).

Do the *P. syringae* need a course in decision making? Well, they seem to be doing all right without one. They appear to know what works for them.

Does decision making operate among other lower life forms as well? What about a flu virus? In its own *knowing* sort of way, does it decide to invade a given body or not to? Does it *know* which organ to infiltrate and which to avoid? And does it decide to flee from antibodies that may attack it? Apparently so.

The Double-Slit Experiment

Added to this, consider the decision making that goes on among particles—not only your particles, but others which are yours for the claiming. Fred Alan Wolf in his book, *Taking the Quantum Leap: The New Physics for Non-Scientists*, describes the well-known double-slit experiment. A stream of subatomic particles is directed toward a screen. A second screen with two long, parallel slits, is "placed between the stream's source and the original screen..., and each particle must pass through one slit or the other in order to reach the final screen." Each time a particle strikes the screen, it leaves a dark spot on it. But, amazingly, if you close one of the slits, "more particles make their way to certain places on the final screen than if you leave both slits open." Particles don't need to be taught how to make decisions. They already know.

'The time has come,' the Walrus said,
'To talk of many things: Of shoes – and
ships – and sealing-wax – Of cabbages
and kings – And why the sea is boiling
hot – ' And whether particles can think.
Adapted from Lewis Carroll

Gary Zukav in his book, *The Dancing Wu Li Masters*, notes that though subatomic particles cannot be considered to be alive by any known measure, they seem to know when to change direction, or polarity. They appear to constantly make certain logical, orderly decisions about their existence. In fact, "more than that, the decisions they seem to make are based on decisions made elsewhere. Subatomic particles seem to know instantaneously what decisions are made elsewhere, and elsewhere can be as far away as another galaxy" (Zukav, p. 72). These infinitesimal particles need no instruction in decision making. Why are we bent, then, on teaching so inborn and fundamental a skill to humans, supposedly the most intelligent creatures of all?

Are Humans Less than the Bugs, Bacteria, and Particles?

Decision making is so simple, so elemental to all forms of matter and energy that it defies description. Yet it remains so complex an operation that it defies total comprehension. It exists as a universal state of knowing, of being in harmony with universe.

You are your own best teacher of decision making as only *you* can know what's right for your life. And you already do. Particles know, snails know, every other living thing knows, and so do you.

What society usually means by *decision making* is that there is a right choice—a correct option about what to do with your life. Such a notion suggests a rational approach. It's as though, when we make life decisions, we should adhere to some sort of printout provided by society's computer. But this logical approach can be used for only about 1 percent of our decision-making efforts. As Buckminster Fuller observed, only 1 percent of universe energy is *visible* (in our human terms), and 99 percent is *invisible*. Therefore, if we rely only on rational, logical, linear decision making, we miss using all of the *invisible* information in our own life-universe.

Somehow, the decision-making process is freely available to all of us without any prescription, licensing, or instructions. We need only realize it's there, tune into it, draw on its limitless energy, trust it, and use it.

Unlimited choices are also available to us—not only *right* moves, but *left* moves. Choosing a combination of both provides us balance throughout life. Some choices may not work out as well as others, but both are vital to move us forward. Buckminster Fuller writes:

> Human beings were given a left foot and a right foot to make a mistake first to the left, then to the right, left again, and repeat. Between the over controlled steering impulses, humans inadvertently attain (between the two) the desired directions of advance. This is not only the way humans work—it's the way the universe works. That is why physics has found no straight lines; it has found a physical universe consisting only of waves (Wagschal, p. 45).

As we veer to the right and left, all we can do is our very best. Abraham Lincoln once said of his life:

> If I were to try to read, much less answer, all the attacks made on me, this shop might as well be closed for any other business. I do the very best I know how—the very best I can; and I mean to keep doing so until the end. If the end brings me out all right, what is said against me won't amount to anything. If the end brings me out wrong, ten angels swearing I was right would make no difference.

11

MOVING FORWARD: UNDERSTANDING THE CULTURAL SHIFTS

Differences

Traditional career uses social context to predict or suggest
what is seen as proper choices for particular outcomes;
Lifecareer uses social context for individual understanding without concern for prediction or
specific result.

A New Civilization Dawns: The Third Wave

We humans experience change so continuously
that we have to be keenly observant of our lives and
of life around us to see specific changes. Today we're
witnessing a vast change in the pattern of life in our
society. So vast that it's changing our very civilization. It's as basic as that.

Though a change in our civilization may seem
awesome, we're able to perceive and understand it

when we let ourselves do so. Consider, for example, Alvin Toffler's analogy of a Third Wave washing the old out to sea and giving rise to the new, more humane civilization now looming on the horizon. This phenomenon is described by Toffler in his book, *The Third Wave,* in which he identifies three different change periods in human history which he calls "waves."

At the beginning of civilization, says Toffler, humans lived chiefly by fishing, hunting, and herding. Then, around 8,000 B.C. the First Wave of change happened—the agricultural revolution which effected the rise of a non-migratory agricultural civilization—which was to continue for thousands of years.

The Second Wave of change—the rise of the industrial civilization as we know it today—started in the mid-1600s. This wave took only 300 years to crest and is now ebbing.

The Third Wave of change—today's post-industrial civilization—began around 1955. With its electronic and high technological capabilities, says Toffler, this wave is likely to affect all of us and could complete itself within a few decades.

Under conditions of electric circuitry, all the fragmented job patterns tend to blend...into...work that more and more resembles teaching, learning, and "human" service...
                    Marshall McLuhan

We live, then, in a most exciting time. We find ourselves at the dawning of the Third Wave. We are the people breathing life into it. As we move into this

compelling new era, we'll not have the luxury of
years to establish cultural guidelines as those before
us did in the Agricultural (First Wave) and Industrial
(Second Wave) periods. The reason is that the current Electronic/High Technology (Third Wave)
period is expected to complete itself within a few
decades. This means we'll have to rely more and
more on our own experience, intelligence, and intuition, not on patterns dictated by others.

The Second and Third Waves and Work Career

During the Industrial period (Second Wave),
production was standardized. Standardization resulted in specialization. Each individual did a specific
job in the process. Each part was part of an un-
changing whole. Timing and sequence became important, in order for the diverse steps to be carried
out at their proper times. Then it grew important to
concentrate factories close to raw materials, labor,
and transportation. Decision making soon was
concentrated in the select few.

In this industrial system, jobs were created for
specific purposes. Young people were trained for
these jobs both on and off site, in special schools, colleges, and universities. What students would find in
the job market could be somewhat predicted. Public
education then took on the task of making students
aware of the world of work. It was the time of the
employee-employer relationship, linked to loyalty
and longer service and individual effort.

Job-market prediction was somewhat possible
because, in the early and mid-1900s, about 250 years
into the Industrial period, work had become somewhat stable. Matching people to jobs gained popularity. Long-term commitment to a job was valued.
Being dependable, punctual, and obedient, and doing

rote/repetitive tasks were all highly valued. They made for a good, stable employee. This meant one didn't move around. "Shiftless" was the word applied to those who didn't stay with a job.

We are the new pioneers.

Children were taught these industrial values at home and at school. They learned how society worked; its habits, its jobs, and how to get those jobs. The popular line then was, "If you want a good job, get a good education." Not everyone abided by it, but few questioned it. There was then, as always, a generation gap. The young often resisted the belief systems of their elders. But, eventually, they found that what they were saying was useful. During this period, traditional values were passed down more readily because it was a somewhat stable time.

Now we're in a new period, the Third Wave. Fritjof Capra, author of *The Turning Point,* suggests that: "We're not in a stable society. We are at the beginning of a very profound cultural transformation. So transmission of the traditional value systems, and the traditional set of ideas, is very problematic." It's problematic because it calls for all of us to start re-evaluating all that we know. Then we have to discard those things that no longer apply. This is a new way of acting.

Further, it isn't easy. We have all grown accustomed to reaching for society's software program, inserting it into our inner computers, and having our directions come to us easily. Now, we're having to write our own programs. And most of us don't feel able to do so. It's like having to start from *go* again. And it's unsettling. But, making it up as we go along can be challenging. We feel a sense of adventure as the pioneers before us did in building a new nation.

We Are the New Pioneers

Early in our nation's history, it took the pioneering settlers months of rugged physical effort to travel across the plains and the mountains—those miles and miles of dry, flat prairie land and almost impossible ranges. There were no maps, no road markers. There were no tour guides, no government grants. There was you—and the wagon, the horses, the rugged stretches of wilderness, the promise. Many people made it. Many didn't. Thanks to those who paved the way, we have graduated from the basic need levels to become the new pioneers. This means that, from here on in, we'll be continually pioneering, if Toffler's judgment is right about the High Technology (Third Wave) period completing itself within several decades.

Toynbee and the Third Wave

The movement from the First to the Second to the Third Waves and from trusting what you're told to what you know can be described in terms of historian Arnold Toynbee's evolution of the cultures of civilizations: a regular pattern of rise, culmination, decline, and disintegration. But, there's something more.

Underlying Toynbee's evolution of cultures is the scientific principle of *dissipative structures.* Marilyn Ferguson in *The Aquarian Conspiracy* described dissipative structures as "...a *flowing wholeness,* highly organized and always in process." Dissipative structures suggest not only a possible winding down of the universe, but an opportunity to grow into greater complexity, through shifts, fluctuations, and upheavals. Critical disturbances can even cause a society to maintain, reorganize to a higher level, or to disintegrate. But, something else rises from each dissipation—life endures in some form.

Disturbances like those we're now experiencing are caused by the Second Wave ebbing and the Third Wave rising powerfully in its wake. These upheavals are shaking up the very depths of a great many people, organizations, and institutions. They make it necessary for them either to reorganize to a higher level or be swept away by the undertow.

From Critical Disturbances, New Ways Are Formed

One new labor approach born of this reorganization is employee leasing. More and more companies are moving to part-time, temporary workers hired through outside agencies. Corporate managers are finding that it saves money. While they may pay a little more per hour to staff up for peak load periods, they don't have full-time salaried workers standing around, adding to their costs, when business is slow. Added to this, the benefits, insurance, and unemployment for temporary workers are all paid for by the leasing company. For business, this approach can end employee benefit and personnel department costs.

Employee leasing also enables a company to hire pre-screened and bonded workers, as needed. This approach allows the temporary workers to choose which assignments they'll take and for how long. It's the new Third Wave way—the *not-tied-to-one-job* way.

Job Security in the Third Wave

If you still believe in job security—maybe because you belong to a labor union—look for more and more unionized companies to find ways around their controls. No contract is invulnerable. Look for more and more companies to go head-to-head with unions. In 1984, the Supreme Court "...adopted new legal standards that make it easier for companies to break their contracts after filing for protection under bankruptcy laws."

In 1983, a large airline company filed for bankruptcy when its maintenance workers struck. With this, the company said it was no longer required to observe its union contracts. Two weeks later, another large airline company tried the same tactic. Its unionized employees took a voluntary pay cut to keep their jobs. The growing move to undermine union strength is making once-powerful unions back down on their demands. One of the large unions, for example, after forcing closure of many small trucking firms by enforcing contracts that call for full-time employees whether the company needed them or not, is now willing to talk to employers about relaxing these rules.

True, labor unions today represent millions of workers. But, as the very nature of work and employment cracks apart like ice under the desert sun, union membership may dwindle, at least in today's types of unions. Universal change is forcing both employers and unions to try new approaches based on cooperation instead of confrontation. The shifting winds of change—propelling our work and our lives in new directions—also are reshaping our organizations and institutions.

Corporate Globetrotting

Many companies today are choosing not to subsidize work careers on a guaranteed basis. This fuels the outmove of already outdated industrial procedures to Third World countries. There, the local labor forces sustain labor-intensive production at lower costs. An example of this, noted earlier, is Atari which moved its assembly-line operations from California to labor-intensive Hong Kong. But, Atari isn't alone.

The *Directory of American Firms Now Operat-*

ing in Foreign Countries shows that more than 3,200
United States corporations have over 21,000 sub-
sidiaries and affiliates in 121 foreign countries.

In the heavily industrialized First World nations,
more production procedures are being mechanized,
automated, computerized, and robotized. This means
the displacement of increasing numbers of more and
more workers, many of whom will move into service
and information-management jobs. It also means that
millions may not be able to find work of any kind. In
Forgewood, England, for example, the unemployment rate is 30 percent. Worse, many young people
there don't expect to ever find work.

Persons at the other end of the age scale are having similar problems in Japan. "Mid-career Jobless-
ness New Japanese Concern," said one recent head-
line. Japan's mandatory retirement at age 60 is causing older men there to have difficulty finding jobs.
One man said his separation pay could cover his
normal living expenses for 10 years. "But what am I
going to do with myself?" he asked. "There's nothing
wrong with my health, and for the sake of staying
healthy, I think I should work." He's right. Human intelligence can't be sent on vacation. It has to create.

Shifting Income Sources:
Steady Lifecareer

As this metamorphosis increases, people every-
where will become more and more accustomed to
part-time work. A recent article by Ron Zemke, in
Training Magazine suggests that in the 1990s fifty
percent of the workforce could be on permanent part-
time employment. Also, a daily-hire, free-lance, work-
here-and-there approach to earning a living and to life
will become a way of life for many people. For all of
us, this means several types of changes: a change in
attitude about work; a change in work habits; a
change in our value system; a change in lifestyle, from

letting someone else make our daily work schedule to making our own; and, a shift to more freedom and creativity. All this adds up to living *Life*-as-career.

Life Does Know What It's Doing

Understand that these changes coming your way aren't enemies. They're opportunities to free yourself and your creativity. It may take you a while, however, to realize and to believe this. As you begin to practice these new principles, your life may take off in an entirely new, surprising, maybe unpredictable direction. You'll find that *life* does know what it's doing.

You don't have to know exactly what you're doing. To start, you don't have to know the result. Trust life.

You may feel it's bad for companies to move jobs abroad or to otherwise deny their workers long-term security. Or you may think it's good that you can be free from 9-to-5 activity that's not meeting your needs. Whatever your views, remember: when you focus on only one aspect, you may miss the others. And what may seem good one moment may in the next moment turn bad.

For example, a farmer owned six handsome horses which his neighbors envied. One morning, he awoke to find his horses gone. When his neighbors heard of this, they exclaimed, "What bad news!"

"How do you know it's bad news?" the farmer asked.

The following morning, his horses returned, bringing with them six wild horses. When his neighbors heard of this, they said, "What good news!"

But, the farmer merely shrugged, "How do you

know it's good news?"

Sure enough, the next morning, the local military commander, needing horses, took them for his troops.

"What bad news!" the neighbors said.

The farmer replied, "How do you know it's bad news?"

The following day, the military commander came back looking for men and recruited all fit young men from the neighboring farms. But, because the farmer had given him his horses, his son was spared.

The neighbors said, "What good news!"

Still, the farmer's only comment was, "How do you know it's good news?" The moral: nothing is good or bad, but your perspective makes it so.

What matters most is how you see the problem. You can't control change, but you *can* control your attitude about it. As the Third Wave overtakes us, we may feel as though we're lost at sea without a lifeboat. We may even think we're drowning. How we come though this depends on our ability to freely flow with and adapt to change. Each of us must do it our own way.

You don't have to know exactly what you're doing either. You don't have to know the result to start. Trust *life.* Rely on your experience, intelligence, and intuition. That's at the heart of the new pioneering. That's living *Life*-as-career.

Waves—Some of Each

How do the First, Second, and Third Waves differ? Take a look:

First Wave: We've just invented the grindstone! Let's find out what to *do* with it.

Second Wave: Let's really put our shoulder to the wheel and our nose to this wonderful grindstone. *Look,* it grinds! If we devote all our energies to it, it'll take *care* of us.

Third Wave: We don't have to turn this darn thing

all day long. It's great to get it going, then sit back, watch it grind, and focus on other things.

Intelligence Evolves

Now you have a better idea of the civilization change currently under way. When you understand change, you can get ahead of it.

To get *ahead* of change, you must look *behind* it somewhat. When you look behind the present Third Wave change in our civilization, what do you see? You see nothing. What's behind the Third Wave change is intelligence. We can't see intelligence. All we can do is have it, feel it, and express it. Intelligence is the energy of universe at work in each of us.

So to get behind the Third Wave change in our civilization, get into your intelligence in two ways: (1) shift your view of science; and (2) shift your view of universe. Since everything is connected, these two are connected as well. To shift your view of science, shift your view of universe. And to shift your view of universe, shift your view of science. So let's review some new science ideas we mentioned in Chapter 4.

Science Today

Isaac Newton, as noted earlier, found what appeared to be a universal truth: the uniform gravitational attraction between two bodies in motion. This appeared to give us humans control in our relationships with nature. Nature seemed to us like one great machine. We started making machines and exploiting their turning of raw materials into substances and products. We standardized. We eagerly entered the Second Wave (industrial) civilization.

But, other things were happening simultaneously in the world of physics. While engineers and technologists were exploiting Newton's principle, physicists were finding microscopic situations in which Newton's principle of uniform attraction didn't apply. And still other physicists were noting the relationship of the observer to the observed as two bodies approached and receded from one another.

As more and more of these exceptions were noted, physicists became increasingly concerned that the basic Newtonian model of mechanics wasn't as universal as originally thought. They started proposing alternate principles of relativity, of quantum mechanics, of self-organizing systems. Therefore, in this century, a change took place in the basic physics model of the universe. Physicists entered a quantum mechanics era.

These quantum principles, some that were cited earlier in this work, operate in all energy/matter relationships. So they have just as much force in ourselves as they do in two particles uniting in mutual attraction.

Among the quantum principles now widely acknowledged and used by modern physicists are the following:

(1)   *The uncertainty principle.* The more you concentrate on the measurement of one factor, the less you know of another or others. Uncertainty is, therefore, introduced. For example, the more you focus on the elements in position, the less you know of their momentum, and vice versa.

(2)   *We find what we look for.* This principle applies in all of our observations. If we look for elements in matter, we find them; if we look for quanta (waves) in matter, we find them.

(3)   *The complementarity principle.* If you change one thing in a system, other things will change throughout the system. A system is a whole.

(4)   *The whole is more than the sum of its parts.* The whole is in each of its parts, but it can't be reconstructed from its parts.

Universe Today

As physicists acknowledged that everything is uncertain, so individuals emerged to judge what aspects of these universal uncertainties to believe. And as physicists came to know that they were creating what they observed, people had to take on a greater personal responsibility for creating their own reality. This was a shift from believing that we could be objective to knowing that subjectivity is all there is. This brought us face-to-face with ourselves.

These changes have moved us into a position where we have to rely more and more upon our own realities, our own intelligence. When you realize this, you come to a more profound understanding of the beauty and responsibility which are yours as a human. In assuming this responsibility, you realize that what happens to another happens to you. Everything is connected.

The movement of intelligence into freer operation within all of us is the evolutionary force powering the movement of our civilization from its Second Wave (industrial) into its Third Wave (post-industrial) condition. This evolution moves us into the Universal Age as well.

The Universal Age is all around us. People are orbiting in space, circling the Earth 14 times in 24 hours. People interrelate with other people in every nation on Earth. And people are continually finding that what formerly has been taken as a boundary can be surmounted when they bring their intelligence into a more comprehensive relationship with nature.

Just as there has been a shift in scientific thought from Newtonian to quantum bases, so we must shift from being Earthbound to being universe citizens. From being nations to being one world. And from being schooled, trained, and packaged for a given career to pursuing our own beckoning *Lifecareers* in the free, unlimiting universe.

12

THE DAWNING OF THE UNIVERSAL AGE

Differences

Traditional career does not address the universal age;
Lifecareer does.

Awakening Our New Potential

As we try to adapt to the Third Wave Civilization, and the world view shift, the dawning of the
Universal Age is also upon us, beckoning us to grow
and go forward with all that it offers.

What is the Universal Age? And what does it
hold for us? At a recent conference, Barbara Marx
Hubbard, author of *The Evolutionary Journey,*
guided those present on the following 15 billion-year
adventure:

Lift-off

Imagine you're lifting off from wherever you

are right this moment. As you gain altitude, and gain the speed of light, you see the northern hemisphere, then planet Earth, then our solar system. Soon, the solar system disappears, like a grain of sand in the water. Now, we're passing through our Milky Way. Then this galaxy disappears. Now, we're in the universe with its billions of galaxies, each composed of billions of stars. Capture for a while this feeling of universal unity and size. This is what exists right now. This is, in the broadest stroke of the universal brush, how it is.

Now come back. Realize from your universal perspective that we mortals are just now popping out of our evolutionary cocoon. We're experiencing a *planetary birth*. We're at the embryonic stage of a planetary system just becoming aware of itself as a whole, interconnected, interdependent system.

We're on the edge of taking responsibility for our citizenship on the planet Earth—a member of solar system Sun, a shining member of galaxy Milky Way. We stand on the edge of our destiny—enlightenment and understanding. We begin to penetrate our universe. We begin to coordinate universe functions as a whole. We awaken to our untapped human potential and the obligations to our universe and to ourselves.

Continuing, author Hubbard chronicles our evolution, from the Big Bang that led to the creation of our solar system and the planet Earth to the appearance of the first hominoids, or pre-humans, nearly 15 billion years later. Carl Sagan, in *Cosmos* suggests this progression:

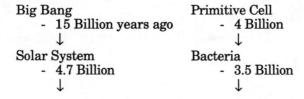

Big Bang
- 15 Billion years ago
↓
Solar System
- 4.7 Billion
↓

Primitive Cell
- 4 Billion
↓
Bacteria
- 3.5 Billion
↓

Green Plants	Vertebrates
- 2 Billion	- 500 Million
↓	↓
Biosphere	Hominoids (Pre-human)
- 1.2 Billion	- 4 Million

As shown here, our material universe is believed to have been formed by a Big Bang some 15 billion years ago. Nearly five billion years later, our solar system appeared, and then, the Earth. The single cell emerged some four billion years ago and achieved a primitive life form a half billion years later. This was followed by the appearance of green plants, then the biosphere, and next, animals. Four million years ago, early pre-humans roamed the earth, looking for food and shelter. Their *Lifecareer* was simple in theory, but tough in practice. You know life is hard when your dinner is as likely to eat you as you, it.

Then after World War II, our generation began experiencing another loop on the evolutionary spiral. That's the *turning point* that Fritjof Capra writes about. It's another turn in nature's vast quest and capacity for quantum transformation to something dramatically new.

If your life form were subatomic particles spread throughout the universe, could you imagine solid material and something as strange as Earth? If you were a molecule floating passively in the seas of early Earth, growing more and more complex, could you imagine life as we know it today?

Each of these leaps in understanding is a quantum jump. And each of these jumps is measured by its quality, not its quantity. Over the eternal eons, gravity and time conspired to fire passing atoms. The merging of this energy is the stuff that became us. I think that's quality. We humans represent universe ever-striving to produce new, whole systems that transcend their parts.

Capacity for Expanded Consciousness

Let's look for a moment at the capacities in our human system right now: personal, social, and technological. Imagine all of them operating fully. The first capacity we know we have is the capacity for expanded consciousness.

There have been and are those among us who have reached through natural means a state of expanded awareness. This state is characterized by the feeling of unity, of oneness. Some call it the God experience. Capra reports that scientists at the leading edge of quantum physics are finding the universe a total interconnection of energy—a Unity. The vision of the universe emerging from the new physics is very similar to the visions, the feelings, the experiences, and the elevated state of consciousness realized through meditation. We are one. The similarities are too great to attribute to mere chance.

For thousands of years, humans have believed they were at the center of things and everything else was separate, out there. Now intellect is reconnecting with creation. On the horizon may be the discovery there's no material world. We're participating in the whole act.

As our consciousness matures, we discover that we can't continue functioning more and more on our own. We must join our energies with those of others, or we'll self-destruct. Our need for inner guidance stimulates our intuition because there's no one to tell us what to do.

Space Shuttle: First Bus to the Infinite

Consider the results and promise of our nation's space program. The space shuttle is the first bus to the infinite. Through the shuttle program, we learned how to manufacture in space. We're now manufacturing a measurement device in space that's far more

accurate than those made on Earth. We also will
build a space platform, our first permanent base in
a formerly totally hostile environment. For manufacturing and construction, we'll learn to use non-
terrestrial resources—lunar or asteroid-mined. This
surge to space is as significant as the first fish-crea-
ture crawling up on land eons ago. That creature
found a hostile planet. Nothing could live on it. But,
tenacious life forms kept crawling out, and gradually, there was life on land.

Now we're ready to create human capabilities in
the extra-terrestrial environment. Soon, we'll leave
Earth to experience living in a strange, hostile place.
We'll stay tethered to our Earth life-support systems
until we become self-sufficient in space. Just as the
first fish that crawled out for a look-see had to return
to the water to breathe, so we'll retain our ties with
Earth. But, as we perfect our artificial life-support
systems in space, as nature changes our human
systems, we'll cut the lifelines to Mother Earth and
head out. Former Earth persons will become true
space-persons. We'll test our infinite human potential.
There's no limit except the limits we create because
of fear and short-sightedness.

Biological Revolution

With the biological/medical revolution, we'll learn
to heal ourselves. We'll come to understand our own
genetic codes. We'll even examine the aging process
and reverse it. We'll become what Buckminster Fuller
called the "continuous human"—a person who lives
on by choice or who dies by choice. With organ
replacements and heart-bypass operations becoming
more commonplace, we have another choice. Do we
pay attention to our bodies and become responsible
for our health, thereby preventing serious health
problems? Or do we ignore preventive health with the
attitude, "Oh, well, it can be replaced"? Our variety of

choices is being radically increased as we prepare to leave our planet. Our choices are increasing as we approach whole-centered consciousness.

Communication Revolution

Next, consider the communication revolution: computers, cybernetics, robotics. The extension of the mind-body system is so profound that we're creating a new form of existence. With robotics, we have the possibility of eliminating most routine work tasks. We can monitor the systems of this Earth to foresee the weather, feed the world, exploit useful economic capabilities. We can enhance the capacity for productivity in our new Earth-space environment through the intelligent extension of our mind-body system. We can approach 100 percent self-suffici–ency for all members of the human race. More important, freeing our creativity will create a universal environment at the dawn of the Universal Age.

Getting On with the Business of Being Fully Human

According to Barbara Marx Hubbard, we may not fulfill our Universal Age destiny in the next 50 years, but we'll experience a major turning point. And when universe reaches such a turning point, it tends to turn willy-nilly. This isn't a metaphor. Our world could turn really tense and topsy-turvy. Those in power, or in search of power, may misuse their powers, particularly regarding nuclear force. Since the U.S. and Russia first squared off in the nuclear power arena, we've felt this tension mounting in the body politic. We're armed for Armageddon.

At the same time, we'll become increasingly aware of our human connectedness. Enough of us will know that we're one, that we're whole, that we're universal, to strive to avoid Armageddon. We'll seek instead to get on with the business of being fully human. We can then begin to realize our *real* potential.

Consider that for several millennia, humanity had to work to survive—and work hard. Men worked in the fields while women were busy keeping house and producing children. For most of human history, people enjoyed no time- and labor-saving conveniences. There was you, a dwelling, and what you could make or do or catch with your hands.

Children didn't spend hours watching television, nor did they spend hours in the local video arcade. They cared for younger brothers and sisters or they worked, helping the family survive. Survival claimed most of early humankind's time, attention, and energy.

Consider, too, that fewer than 1 percent of the world's people in 1900 enjoyed an adequate, pleasing standard of living. By contrast, in 1980, 60 percent (and this percentage continues to increase) enjoyed a standard of living higher than that once reserved for royalty and other persons of wealth.

Abraham Maslow's hierarchy of needs suggests that certain basic needs must be met in our lives. Once our food, shelter, security, safety, and self-esteem needs are met, we need growth and development. This need then becomes as basic a drive as the need for food and shelter.

If Maslow's theory is correct, today there's an unprecedented drive for growth and development world-wide. This is a new and exciting phenomenon that can benefit us all.

The Universal Age and Lifecareer

The Universal Age marks a quantum jump in evolution. It's the going to and living in space. It's all the opportunities that now exist for everyone to make it. It's also the fact that we're all gradually being freed from dehumanizing labor. This means that more people than ever before now have the time to consider what they want to create and give to the world.

Life does know what it's doing.

The dawning of the Universal Age heralds the living of *Life*-as-career. We're moving from trust in job and employer to trust in *life* and self. As we realize that *life does know what it's doing,* we come to rely more and more on our inner messages and values. In doing so, we acknowledge there are no experts, no one who knows more than we do in regard to our Lifecareer. And, as we become attuned to ourselves, we become more open to information in universe. The exciting part is that if the holographic theory is accurate, i. e., that each small part of the universe contains a complete picture of the whole in it, then, since we're a part of universe, we have access to more information than we ever imagined. This affords us even more possibilities.

We also come to see that career is whole: just as there are no straight lines in universe, so there are no straight lines for career. Similarly, there are no right or wrong decisions in career. Each decision brings us more information upon which to base our next decision, and learn more about ourselves. Added to this, we come to realize there's nothing wrong in doing what we love. We also know that, if the job seems difficult, and we feel like we're working, that's not what we want to do for long. We want to fuller—that is, use our energy joyfully—not work. When we fuller, we feel whole. And we want to feel increasingly whole, fulfilled, and joyful. So we decide to be *fullers*. The Industrial Age person was a worker. The

Universal Age person is a *fuller*.

Joseph Campbell, in his book *The Power of Myth,* suggests that humanity is not seeking the meaning of life. He says:

> I think that what we're really seeking is an experience of being alive, so that our life experience on the purely physical plane will have resonances within our own innermost being and reality, so that we actually feel the rapture of being alive.

That's the *fullering* experience.

13

THE NEW PIONEERING CHALLENGE

Differences

Traditional career suggests that career is made; Lifecareer suggests career is lived and becomes the path you leave behind.

How It Is

As we leave the Second Wave, enter the Third Wave, and experience the dawning of the Universal Age, we find ourselves:

    (a) having a crisis of perception;
    (b) dealing with Society's *they*;
    (c) trying to release useless fear;
    (d) practicing being nobody but ourselves;
    (e) checking out the results (not for approval, but for information); and
    (f) trying to keep our livelihoods

together in the midst of rapid
change from a manufacturing to
an information/service society.

Each of us has to deal with these conditions in his
or her own unique way. You'll also find as you search
for your purpose that you *seem* to make much of the
journey alone. But it's amazing how many of your
friends are experiencing the same feelings. They just
don't talk about them. "Why is it that everyone else
seems so together?" a client asked recently. Another
client wonders why her plan isn't working although
she's perfectly clear about what she wants to do.
Each of us has our individual struggles and challenges.

A Crisis of Perception

As we move further into the Universal Age, we
find new potential in a world view that's shifting
from fragmentation to wholeness. For the first time,
each of us is beginning to get a glimpse of the enor-
mous power within us. We know it isn't power over,
but power *with*. We realize with Marshall McLuhan,
author of *The Medium is the Massage*, that: "There
are no passengers on Spaceship Earth. Everyone's
crew."

Being crew isn't easy when you're used to sitting
back and leaving the driving to others. As new pioneers in the Universal Age, there are no chauffeurs—
we're *all* drivers. For many, this may bring on what
Fritjof Capra calls a crisis of perception:

Today our society as a whole finds itself
in a state of crisis. This is what we perceive when we watch the news on television or when we read the newspapers.
We hear about our economic crisis, an
environmental crisis, an armament crisis,

a rising wave of violence and crime, a
crisis in health care, and so on. I believe
that these are just different facets of one
and the same crisis. It's essentially a crisis
of perception. Like the crisis in physics at
the beginning of the century, it comes
from the fact that we're trying to apply
the concepts of an outdated world view
to solve the major problems of our time
(p. 5, 1983).

The outdated view cited here by Capra is the
Newtonian-Cartesian theory that the world is
mechanistic and works much the same way as a
clock. Therefore, if you have all the parts, you have
the whole. The new view of the world is more
wholistic and interconnected. It holds that the whole
is *greater* than the sum of the parts.

When you think about what in a society keeps
you from acting on *Life*-as-career, you realize it's no
one thing. It's a vast number of things, all invisibly
interconnected. Some of these invisible threads are
now becoming visible, particularly in the work area,
they're things we've taken for granted—longevity of
jobs, availablity of attractive jobs, worker-employer
alliance (showing up for work, doing the job, and receiving a paycheck), and our own need to grow.
Stability in all those areas has had a tendency to
freeze personal development. That is, little disturbance, little growth.

However, all that is becoming unglued and it's
changing our lives. For instance, work cycles are
much shorter necessitating more job searches of one
kind or another; fewer jobs are considered attractive
in terms of pay; and a switch from one-size-fits-all to
customization in organizations, which is forcing
employees to think in terms of a customized life.
These multiple changes are forcing many to grow at

rates not dreamed possible several years ago and this is causing a crisis of perception which is affecting other areas of life. This is very different from only having to learn the conventional wisdom of the day and start doing it. Even more unsettling, we now have to customize, that is, write many of our own rules.

Now the flip side of the coin is this: it's possible that we're suffering a crisis of perception about ourselves. Even if there were no disturbances around work/finances, there could be a crisis of perception in personal growth. Consider Pat's situation. She said to herself, "I'll work six years on my project, then I'll get a teaching job." She had a Ph.D. and an impressive vita and that sounded like a very good plan. She worked six years on her project, finished it, and began to look around for a teaching job. Guess what? She found a few, but none in her specialization. One of the potential jobs looked very interesting, but because she had spent six years on her project and had had very different experience, they wouldn't consider her. So, here was Pat, a Ph.D., with a 20 page vita, several outstanding awards, and her wonderful plan of teaching not possible.

In thinking about the situation, she said, "I've grown myself beyond what is happening in my field now." This was quite startling to her because she had not anticipated this problem. As she looked back she could see that her decision to commit 6 years to her project had changed her life. "I think that is Life's way of keeping me on track with my mission because had I known then what I know now, I may have been too scared to commit. However, Life protected me from myself."

One-Size-Fits-All Gives Way to Customization

The notion that *everyone is crew* is now surfac-

ing in business organizations. It's no longer them and
us, it's we. We are equal; we are one. The organization's response to this can be seen in the HayGroup's
1988 Environmental Scan. Some of their observations are:

• Employment contracts are being replaced with
working arrangements, customized by each organization's particular value structure, market conditions,
worker requirements, and technology capabilities.
• Preconceived notions about the employer-
employee relationship must be abandoned.
• New multiple work arrangements, to customize for wide-ranging needs of work force seg-
ments, will replace the one-size-fits-all.
• The most significant change will be the continued participation of women in the work force.
• Thinking of one work force must be discarded,
because of special needs created by worker sex, eth-
nic heritage, educational or skill level, age, or other
factors.

The HayGroup reports the 1987 Yankelovich
poll which divided the adult population into five sectors: (1) preservers [19%]; (2) anglers [24%];
(3) contenders [14%]; (4) new establishment [20%];
and (5) framers [23%]. This diversity will present
new challenge to organizations and will be com-
pounded as organizations expand globally to other
lands and cultures.
With the emerging sectors, the traditional employment alliance, for all practical purposes, has
been run through the shredder. That alliance was
supported by a stable, competitive external business
environment, rapid market growth, and employees
who shared common values. However, that alliance
seems to have gone the way of the time clock, and
new understandings are emerging.

The Working Arrangement

The new understanding will be viewed more as a social alliance than an employment contract, and will consider worker lifestyles. It'll be called a *working arrangement*—"a loose, tacit, two-way understanding designed for an environment with no guarantees, and where neither side has the upper hand. This Arrangement will be characterized by its fluidity." It'll be worked out on an individual and group basis, depending on need. Customization will be its trademark.

The movement of career-ownership from the organization to the individual via work arrangements and the customization of life are major emerging forces.

The HayGroup, 1988

The new Arrangement won't govern the employee-employer relationship, but it'll present a framework for choice. In the Arrangement, a good job will be expected, but it'll be defined more broadly than it was under the employment alliance, where a good job meant income security through steady work, decent levels of pay, safe working conditions, opportunities for advancement, vacation, and retirement plans. More important, under the employment alliance, there was an implicit understanding that the *good job* wouldn't create headaches like frequent or unexpected demands for learning new skills or achieving higher levels of performance.

The Arrangement will start with the understanding that learning new skills and higher levels of performance will be an *integral part* of the relationship. The benefits—steady work, decent pay, opportunities for advancement, etc.—will now be linked directly to an employee's ability to respond to ongoing demands for competitive performance.

The Shift

While employees will be asked to abandon any expectations of job *security* as defined under the employment alliance, they'll be participating more directly in shaping the direction of the organization. And if improved performance should result from their efforts, they'll have the opportunity to share more directly in the rewards (profits).

The shift is from employees *working hard, working well, and working anonymously* to recognizing that their *destiny is tied* to *how the organization fares*. Loyalty, sticking around, and staying out of trouble are giving way to actively participating in the business efforts and accepting the outcomes, good and bad.

Some questions now for companies appear to be:

> • To what extent and how should employment and pay be linked to company performance?

> • Will the work force be bought (temporary) or made (permanent)? Which functions will be done in-house and which contracted out?

> • What should be the prime considerations: equity issues or the values of a differentiated work force?

> • Should corporate culture promote

uniformity or recognize diversity of
work force? (HayGroup, 1988)

A few of the work innovations being considered
are cross-training, problem-solving groups, flextime,
permanent part-time jobs, project-based organizations, job enrichment, management training, com-
pressed work week, formal job rotation, job sharing,
and work-at-home.

Customization of Life

All the Yankelovich groups (anglers, framers,
preservers, new establishment, and contenders) were
asked if they agreed with the statement, "There's no
right or wrong way to live." The lowest percent of
agreement was in the Preserver Group with 27 percent, while the highest level of agreement was in the
Angler group with 89 percent. However, generally
70 percent of all the groups agreed there is no right
or wrong way to live.

The customization of life seems a high priority
for most of the work force. The working through of
this customization will have many glitches and barriers, but will ultimately bring great reward. For the
persistent, the outcomes will be exciting. Those able
to customize their lives will find the new working arrangements in business much to their liking with
great potential for growth.

Clearly, the movement of career-ownership
from the organization to the individual via work
arrangements and the customization of life are major
emerging forces. Both of these forces supports and
encourages all of us to live Life-as-Career which
means living life on our own terms.

Resistance Won't Help You
Ride the Third Wave

If you dig in your heels and resist considering

life as a creative force in career (i.e. remain a preserver), you're apt to find yourself dispensable when
you no longer add to the profits on your employer's
balance sheet.

Today, technology, reorganization, and belt
tightening are relieving more people of work than
red ink. John, a college junior, knows this well. His
father had worked for a large bank for 30 years. One
day, the bank gave his father the option of moving
across country to the main office or retiring. He
chose retirement.

This incident has had a strong effect on John's
work-career direction. He has a first-hand example
of nothing being certain, even when an employee
gives a major part of his or her life to a company.
You can't account for nor predict a company's
changing position. Those who are running it think
one way one day, based on current information, and
another way the next. So, John has decided to major
in entrepreneurship in college and in finance. He
eventually wants to have a small business of his own.

Already, John is looking around to determine
what it might be. He's trying to identify what he enjoys and loves to do. He's exploring activities that
might generate income for him. His father's advice to
him is, "Make sure that, when you give your life to a
company, you're *choosing* to do it. And when it no
longer feels right, get out. Don't worry what they'll
think. When *they* put you out, they won't worry
about what *you* think." This response is typical of the
old employer-contract model where loyalty was
expected and with it came a guarantee of income for
a long time. Being part of the old employment alliance set up expectations that eventually couldn't be
met, so it caused employee frustration and anger.

The Sisyphean Task

Camus, in *The Myth of Sisyphus*, tells about

Sisyphus who was condemned by the gods to roll a heavy stone to the top of a steep mountain. As he neared the top, the stone, because of its great weight, rolled down again, forcing him to jump out of the way to avoid being crushed. This is akin to what many people are doing in their lives today. They try to roll the old rules to the top of life's mountain (embrace outdated conventional wisdom). Being unable to hold them up there (finding it no longer applies), they jump out of the way and watch the old rules simply roll back down again. Then, they roll them back up, again and again.

Another strategy would be to forget those rules and heavy stones and start understanding the new working arrangement. If you choose to work for someone else, consider making a work of your own, too. If you choose permanent part-time employment or self employment, then make your own rules. After all, this is the age of customization, not just in products and in businesses, but in your own personal life.

In losing your job, for example, you may feel that the runaway stone of security is ready to crush you. You may feel you no longer have a way to achieve your aims. Now you'll never reach the high ground, you tell yourself. But keep in mind: even the high ground isn't solid and secure. Like life, it's undergoing constant change. Try instead to see the *high ground* as something we live, not as something we reach, conquer, and stand on—and certainly not as somewhere we spend a lifetime. Set your intentions and then get out of your own way. You don't have to push a heavy load. Just remember that the top of the mountain isn't *up there*. It's right where you are *now*. An interviewer asked Phillip Michael Thomas, one of the lead actors in the television show, *Miami Vice*, "When was the best time in your life?" He replied, "Now." He said, "Yesterday is a cancelled check, tomorrow a promissory note, and today is 'cash in hand'."

The Torch Has Been Passed
(From the Employment Contract to the Working Arrangement)

As the Third Wave approaches, some people will react with confusion and pain, fearing their basic needs won't be met. Others may still expect some company to take care of them, unaware that during the Third Wave, the employment contract is being replaced with the working arrangement, which changes things from predictability to no guarantees. Many employees are already being faced with this change. Many don't know what to do next because it's a new way of thinking, with new responsibilities and new learnings.

Just as the new *working arrangement* in organizations will include frequent and unexpected demands upon employees to learn new skills and achieve higher levels of performance, so will the employee find the same demands made on him in his personal life, because nothing will be assured, and new ways of bringing in more income will need to be devised.

Hence, more attention will be given to personal finances as assured income goes by the wayside. Those living a year or two ahead of their income will have the opportunity to rethink that strategy or live the consequences of it. Moving from hard income (assured monthly salary) to soft income (free lance, and maybe permanent part-time employment) will call for skills and performance that weren't needed in the old lifestyle of employer contract.

The movement to permanent part-time work will make unexpected demands on the family; it'll give each family member the opportunity to rise to a higher level of performance personally than has formerly been necessary. Permanent part-time work will also encourage creating a supplemental work of your own.

The Age of Customization or:
I Did It My Way

An employer recently told of a man who had applied to him for a top management job. Instead of sending a resume with his application, the man merely dropped him a note that said, "Call me to talk about the job."

The employer phoned the applicant and asked the applicant to send in a resume. The applicant replied that he would rather *talk* about the job—and his qualifications.

To this, the employer said that he didn't have time to talk then. The applicant responded by saying that he wouldn't send a resume. Both thanked one another, and the conversation ended. But, the applicant had the courage to define how he wanted to be selected. And the employer retained the option of accepting or rejecting the approach. The important thing is each did it the way he wanted to. That's the new model/paradigm—customization.

On a Clear Day You Can See—
Well, Almost Forever

Once you're able to understand the Third Wave civilization, you'll recover from your *crisis of perception.* You'll also gain new insight. You'll realize that what society is experiencing is a quantum leap in its understanding. The industrial mentality of one-size-fits-all no longer holds. It's been replaced by customization, diversification, variety, and multiple possibilities. This is an atmosphere where you can begin to practice being nobody but yourself which means living *life on your own terms.*

14

WHAT KEEPS YOU FROM ACKNOWLEDGING THAT LIFE-IS-CAREER?

Differences

Traditional career supports following theories by leading theorists; Lifecareer believes that each individual is his or her own theorist.

Life is our career. Down deep, each of us knows that. So why do we avoid acting upon it? Why do we lack faith? And why are we afraid to just let go, to just let our intuitions guide us? Let's take a look at some key reasons for our resistance.

Separating Ourselves from Universe

Our main reason for resisting is that we do not believe we are part of the universe. We see universe (out there) and us (down here). And we don't tend to see the connection. We, therefore, find it difficult to think of ourselves as being subject to the same principles as universe. For example, many still believe that *objectivity* is possible. We have Isaac Newton and René Descartes to thank for that. Their theories suggested that we all could be objective and separate ourselves from the phenomena around us.

In the early 1900s, however, scientific thinking changed dramatically. Einstein and many other scientists shifted to a different view. Their concepts reshaped the ways we perceive universal laws at work. As a result, today our world view is deeper and broader than that of Newton or Descartes. While this new scientific picture of the world still includes their views, it expands our understanding of the infinite time-space dimension in which we live—in fact, to the very limits of our comprehension. It also puts universe and nature back into us and vice versa.

How does this change things for you? When you see yourself as part of nature and it as part of you, you realize it's possible that you can now gain entry to all information in universe. You gain access to that information as your faith about it increases. A recent client was willing to do this and see what happened. "I learned I was getting what I wanted," she said later. "When I changed my mind, my life changed."

Her life changed because she changed her mind. Now this isn't something mystical or extraordinary. It's happening every day to ordinary people. Sure, they're surprised and sometimes even amazed. They're also excited about their new freedom and power.

Would you like to know more? Well, for one thing, not being part of something tends to make you believe that you don't know what's happening. You feel alone, apart, and different. So you tend to take others' advice about what you need to do because you don't trust your own impulses and intuitions. You think you can't, you shouldn't, you mustn't, you won't. You also think someone else will do it (whatever that is) better than you, so you let them. The sad part is that *they* don't know what to do either; *they* see only their own realities. Knowing that your intuition is as good as anyone else's is a big step forward. When you take this step, you also take your experience, intelligence, and intuition out of moth balls and start to use them regularly.

Pianist Ursula Oppens, winner of the prestigious Avery Fisher Prize in music, felt that she knew herself better than anyone else. Of her career as a concert pianist, Oppens recalls: "Although I'd played the piano all my life, I wasn't sure I wanted to be a pianist. I went to Radcliffe's career counseling, and they told me that as an English major, I had three choices: One, I could go to graduate school, if I was very good. Two, I could get a master's in teaching if I was almost good. And if I didn't want to do either of those, I could learn typing and shorthand. I was furious...but I thought if it's going to be typing, then I really do play the piano better than that" (Harvard Magazine, p. 91). She realized she had to act on what she knew about herself.

Let go of the notion that you are separate from the universe. Enjoy and use the full power of universe. Doing so will help you realize more and more that your *Life* is your career. As Buckminster Fuller observed:

> The greatest challenge facing...(people) today is that of responding and conforming only to their own most delicately insistent intuitive awarenesses of what the truth seems to them to be as based on their own experiences and not on what others have interpreted to be the truth regarding events that neither they nor others have experienced-based knowledge (Wagschal p. 142).

It's Not Always Popular to Admit You Live Life-As-Career

Another reason we resist fully living *Life*-as-career is that it isn't always popular to do so. Thus, many people wait for it to become popular. Then it will be safe to admit that *Life*-is-career. We may even shout it! Look around you. How many people do you know who, when asked what they do for a living, say, "Live"? None probably. Surely, you don't want to be the first one to say that. People might think you're daffy if you talk about *Life*-as-career. They may even ask, "What do you mean? What are you talking about?" After all, most people today still regard career as a job, not as an attitude about life. So anyone who embraces this new view is bound to be misunderstood by some. But don't worry about that. It's better to be misunderstood than to revert to old ideas. While we're misunderstood, we keep learning and growing. And we have good company as more and more people take that road.

But, some people are still caught up in old thought. Book publishers, for example, publish, promote, and sell books about careers in business, industry, nursing, music, and so on. They still refer to career as job. Similarly, school counselors help students to *choose a career*. They mean *find a job*—a job you can hold onto as long as possible.

However, holistic professionals will tell you the following:

Find the type of work you like. Do what feels right to you, and try to make your living from it. If you take a job and then find you don't like it, move on—try something else. Nowhere is it written that life demands you find a job and stick with it just because you have it. Remember, *Life* is your career.

If you find someone who says things like this, he or she really knows life and can help you.

Most public school guidance programs talk about *knowing yourself,* but mostly it's about matching that knowing with a job as known by *them.* Matching may be part of finding right work, but it isn't the first consideration. In finding right work, you may end up doing something you didn't think you could do. Matching may happen, but you don't have to start that way.

Since most people still believe in this approach, however, talking about Life-as-career may mark you as *different.* And people who are *different* often find society a tough row to hoe.

Comedian Jonathan Winters, for example, quit school to join the Marines. His geometry teacher warned him against not finishing his studies. But, Winters did what he felt was right for him at the time—he dropped out. His success as a comedian wasn't affected by his lack of knowledge about geometry.

You Don't Always Honor Your Own Career Theory

Another reason you may *not be* living Life-as-career is that you're trying to live your life based on someone else's theory *of career*—the *ought*s and *shoulds* that bombard everyone.

The there you think is there may not be there when you get there.

You've probably always accepted and stuck to the common career development beliefs, not giving them a second thought. They're part of the industrial thinking that permeates our society. You are, therefore, not encouraged to consider and use your personal career theory. Rather, you are led to believe that someone else knows what's best for you.

If you have any doubt that you subscribe to these beliefs, ask yourself the following:

As you moved along in life, did you...

- do what others thought was right for you?
- act on their *You should go to college* advice?
- buy into their *You should develop this skill, or that one*?
- wear the right suit to the job interview?
- listen to what *they* said were the right moves to *make it* in your work career?
- accept *their* views of what success is?

These questions are deeply rooted in *someone else's* theory of career development. Everyone around you can provide wonderful advice on how to get there from here. But, you cannot get there from here because there is no *there*. It's only an illusion. *The there you think is there may not be there when you get there.*

What exists is only an eternal *here*—the present— the only time in which you can ever truly live. There is nowhere to go. You are there. And if you make the most of *now*, the future will take care of itself.

Please Don't Save Me from My Experience; I Need It

Another reason you may not *fully* live Life-as-career is that all the experts try to save you from your experiences. Counselors try to save their counselees. Professors, their students. Employers, their employees. Spouses, their spouses. Parents, their children. And the list continues on endlessly. What these people don't realize is that *saving* people from their experience is worse than physically robbing them. Instead, they try to justify it with *because I love you*, or *it's for your own good*. Parents constantly try to save children from the pain and pressures of growing up. What they do is deny their children most of their learning experiences. Yes, it's painful to watch children struggling to overcome problems and pitfalls. But, it's how they grow.

Oysters don't make pearls without experiencing pain. Growth can be the same. From our struggles comes growth. We all know that life starts with a struggling, traumatic experience: birth. We are thrust from the warmth and safety of the womb into the cold, noisy, frightening world *out there*. Each time we face and deal with a problem, we gain strength for the next one. To intervene and try to save a child from these experiences, denies his or her birthright. Every experience a child has offers the opportunity to learn and grow.

However, we do everything possible to protect them from life's trials. We do it in the name of love. But, love is letting another live his or her own life. It isn't intervening every time a dark cloud hovers. We all have to live our own lives, even as children.

This is not to say that children should be allowed to wander unchecked into dangerous situations. At times, they need to be taken by the hand and guided to safety. Other times, we need only to draw them maps and let them find their own way.

To differentiate between actual danger and painful growing problems is the key. Often, we just have to trust our instincts and intuition and take a chance.

We (and our children) must come to realize that our life-experiences provide critical information that helps us to survive and succeed in future missions. Each of us, then, needs our experiences to live our life. If we are saved from them, we are denied learning and growth.

Fear of Looking Foolish

Another reason you may avoid fully living *Life*-as-career is that you just don't trust yourself and are afraid you'll look foolish to others. Noted neurosurgeon Karl Pribram hasn't let concerns like these hinder his research efforts. He's been criticized by more conventional neuroscientists for his bold speculations and for seizing upon new findings outside his field in order to understand memory. Pribram recalls the remark of pioneer memory researcher Ewald Hering which suggests that every scientist begins to be interested in his work and what his findings mean.

> Then he has to choose. If he starts to ask questions and tries to find answers, to understand what it all means, he'll look foolish to his colleagues. On the other hand, he can stop trying to understand what it all means; he won't look foolish, and he'll learn more and more about less and less. You have to decide to have the courage to look foolish (Wilber, p. 19).

Our natural tendency as humans is to complete ourselves. For Pribram, this included going outside his field and risking criticism from his colleagues. But, he was doing what he needed to do then to complete his understanding. Without that type of courage, he probably would not have done all that he has.

Not Trusting Your Career Compass

Another reason you may not be fully acting on Life-as-career is that you don't trust your Career Compass. Acknowledging your Career Compass readings which come from your experience, intelligence, and intuition, can give you more information than you'll ever have lifetimes to use.

Author Peter McWilliams chose to do what felt right, following his Career Compass, when he decided to self-publish his first book. McWilliams had been snubbed earlier when he tried to market his light-hearted computer manuscript to publishers. "Nobody's interested in computer books," McWilliams was told at the time, "and even if they were, they wouldn't be interested in funny ones."

After most publishing houses rejected his work, McWilliams started his own small publishing business. His first book not only sold, but sold so well that he followed it with others. Today, the computer expert who's reported not to know a lick of programming and dropped out of Eastern Michigan University at age 19, is a best-selling author several times over.

This same principle works in *Lifecareer.* If you let go, then you can experience the full range of life's possibilities. Otherwise, a struggle for control rages within you. Your logical, reasoning self tries to wrestle your intuition down on the mat at every decision point. And intuition, though not an active combatant, exerts a constant pressure that you can't ignore. That's because it's your own inner knowing, telling you how you feel about things. It tells you what's really in your heart.

Feeling separate from universe, not admitting you live Life-as-career, not honoring your own career theory, letting others save you from your

experience, fear of looking foolish, and not trusting
your Career Compass are just a few of the barriers to
living Life-as-Career.

Below make your own list of things that keep
you from fully living Life-as-Career:

1. _____

2. _____

3. _____

4. _____

5. _____

6. _____

PART IV

TECHNIQUE AND LIFECAREER

15

HOW DO YOU ADVANCE YOUR LIFE-AS-CAREER?

Differences

Traditional career focuses on career planning; Lifecareer on Career Compassing.

The Career Compass

Throughout this book, I have mentioned the Career Compass, and in this chapter I would like to discuss it more in depth.

First, why use the words "Career Compass"? Because the compass is an ideal symbol for the concept. According to the dictionary, a *compass* is a device for determining directions by means of a freely rotating needle that indicates magnetic north. The Career Compass, then, is a personal device for determining one's career directions by means of an internal needle that freely turns on the combined information obtained from one's own experience, intuition, and intelligence.

Second, many people find the term "Career Compass" useful in helping them to think about the combined results of experience, intelligence, and intuition in their life. (If this term doesn't work for you, come up with one on your own.) It really doesn't matter what term you use; it's simply important that experience, intelligence, and intuition not be regarded as separate, but as a working unit—constantly being drawn magnetically toward one's life mission. An example of separate thinking is the phrase, "Intuitively, I feel I should..." or "My intuition tells me that...." However, it isn't intuition alone, but the combined results of experience, intelligence, and intuition that point us toward our next steps in life. So, I use the term "Career Compass" to underscore the unity of experience, intelligence, and intuition as a potentially powerful force in our lives.

Whatever view of reality deepens our sense of the tremendous issues of life in the world wherein we move, is for us nearer the truth than any view which diminishes that sense.
                    W. R. Inge

The final reason I emphasize the Career Compass is that breaking away from ties to conformity and becoming more self-aware, (that is, recognizing we can make choices) requires more frequent use of the Career Compass. In conformity, there usually is little need to use your Career Compass as someone else has figured things out for you and you generally act on that finding. However, when one becomes self-aware, there is less attention to conventional wisdom and more focus on one's own knowledge. I'll explain more about these levels of development later in this chapter.

The Purpose of the Career Compass

The Career Compass is your inner guide in your life unfoldment. Career Compassing is a more powerful activity than Career Planning because it's neither time nor content bound. It's not confined to life-direction information. Career Compassing wraps itself around your entire life movement anywhere and at any time. The Career Compass is your life kaleidoscope. It tumbles around in random orderliness (looking random but falling into an orderly pattern). When it stops momentarily, a pattern is formed and then it's off to another tumble and another pattern. With each tumble or turn of the kaleidoscope, events fall into different patterns. Furthermore, how things fall isn't predetermined. The Career Compass has no expectations. Therefore, you don't have to spend time wondering what will happen. You simply know a pattern will be formed.

When you make it a point to listen to your Career Compass, you'll start to receive useful information, and you will have plenty of time to set in motion the necessary pieces. Just remember that life's pieces are only temporarily set. Then the Career Compass spins again, scanning for more information, external or internal. When it stops, it provides another reading which may modify the prior one. The main purpose of the Career Compass is to help you do what you uniquely came into the world to do.

Experience

Experience is the first element of the Career Compass. In starting to write about something I think is so commonly understood—or should be, I'm re-

minded of the different ways some children interpret
the reason for their time-out discipline schedules.
One child will love the concept and think it's a grand
idea to see who has the least number of time-out
minutes at the end of the month. Another child will
wonder "Why do this?" So in regard to explaining
what is meant by *experience* here, some people
probably will have no trouble understanding what
the term means, while others will wonder about it.
This section is for those who want a little more ex-
planation.

There are two kinds of experience: internal and
external. External experience is what happens in everyday life. It's that good day we had or that miser-
able one, it's what we accomplished, it's how our
bodies felt, and it's our relationships. All these things
give us content for our internal experience. It's our
internal experience that tends to keep us busy
thinking. That is, we're constantly comparing our
outer experience with our inner experience, and our
sense of well-being is based on how well those two
match.

When there isn't a feeling of *match* between our
outer and inner experience, we can run into problems. And this shows up frequently in many aspects
of our life, particularly in life direction.

It's also true that two people can experience the
same thing yet have completely different perceptions
of it. I'm reminded of two sisters who visited their
grandmother one summer. They traveled by train.
Afterward, the sisters were talking and one said,
"Wasn't it fun, riding the train?" The other replied, "I
thought it was horrible. I hated it." It's all a matter of
perception and interpretation.

The same thing is true for life direction. From
time to time, most of us have experiences we don't
like. Some have more of these experiences than others. But, how these experiences are interpreted is all

that's important. If a person interprets an experience as negative and then feels victimized by it, there will be little opportunity to learn from it. People who feel like victims of their experiences usually don't believe that life works because they interpret *working* to mean working *right;* what they don't realize is that, even when life moves left, it's *working.*

On the other hand, the person who sees a negative experience as a learning opportunity has the chance to develop a better attitude which can advance the learning process. This means he or she may not undergo any depression nor have physical reactions in response to the imprint of negative feelings. Such persons tend to have more confidence and energy because they know they can be choiceful about their experiences. This often leads them to realize that they also can be choiceful about the feedback they receive which can improve their overall feelings about experience and its effects on the Career Compass.

For example, most of us have had some negative experience with family members or friends that gave us a feeling of *not being good enough.* Some people felt this more intensely than others. However, we have a better chance of feeling good about ourselves, maintaining a positive outlook, when we can be choiceful about what kinds of feedback (both positive and negative) we receive and whether we want to receive it at all. These are important options to know about as negative feedback can erode confidence and turn a "go for it" outlook into a "what's the use?" feeling.

Sometimes negative feedback is transmitted in a joking way. We all know people who use humor to convey or soften their real feelings. This can give us an experience that is either neutral or negative.

Still other people think they are doing us a favor by telling us what someone else thinks of us, and they tend to do this in a very nice way. While some people can ignore this type of negative input, for others it can take days or even weeks for the information to pass out of awareness. Meanwhile, this input alters our experience of ourselves and changes our Career Compass readings which, in turn, affect our life direction. It also can undermine our motivation, confidence and general well-being.

In studying the lives of certain great leaders, I found they apparently possessed the ego strength to be able to sustain considerable negative experiences and still go on. This may be due to their ability to interpret their negative experiences in positive ways, at least positive enough to enable them to keep pursuing their dreams. For instance, consider the aspiring politician who had the following record for left turns:

Failed in business	1831
Defeated for Legislature	1832
Second failure in business	1833
Suffered nervous breakdown	1836
Defeated for Speaker	1838
Defeated for Elector	1840
Defeated for Congress	1843
Defeated for Senate	1855
Defeated for Vice President	1856
Defeated for Senate	1858
Elected President	1860

That politician was Abraham Lincoln. He is an example of deliberate Lifecareering—living life full-out—and Career Compassing with courage and confidence.

Intelligence

Intelligence is the second element of the Career Compass. Intelligence (at a different level) exists throughout our entire body, not just in our brain/

mind, or we couldn't survive. Why? Fritjof Capra, author of *The Turning Point*, notes that for self organization to occur, some kind of mental activity has to take place. Scientifically then, there appears to be an intelligence of sorts in our body cells. Therefore, if we use only brain/mind intelligence, we overlook a large percentage of the intelligence available to us. In practical terms, this means we can bring all of our intelligence to bear on any problem, not just that in the brain/mind. To start, acknowledge that intelligence isn't merely from the neck up.

Intuitions often turn dreams into demonstrable facts.
Buckminster Fuller

Intuition

Intuition is the third element of the Career Compass. It is that which is already known, knowledge coming through the body or from the brain/mind. It's that flash that comes seemingly from nowhere. It is that which we know profoundly, but have no particular reason to know.

Buckminster Fuller, in his book *Intuition,* wrote that he considered his intuition his most important faculty, even though he admitted it wasn't a quality that had always been highly regarded.

Fuller tells the story of Professor F. S. C. Northrop at Yale University and another educator at a different university. Both men, without knowledge of each other's work, were engaged in searching the personal papers of three great scientists who had made some breakthrough discoveries in the physical sciences. The professors examined the scientists' personal letters and research notes as well as letters received by the scientists from relatives and close friends around the time they made their most significant discoveries.

Both professors found that the single most important factor aiding these scientists in making their breakthrough discoveries was what they called their "first and second intuitions." The first intuition was identified as a sudden, strange impulse to look in this or that direction when one is already occupied in a different direction. The second intuition, which the professors found usually surfaced immediately after the scientists had made their respective discoveries, was identified as a sudden insight signaling what needs to be done *right now*. Such an intuition might be, "Don't go out to lunch. Sit down right now and write the documentation of the discovery." Evidence of these first and second intuitions was found in the diaries of all three scientists. Fuller suggests that Professor Northrop's research on the three noted scientists powerfully reaccredited the intuition function among the scientific intellectuals.

On a simpler level, think about your personal interactions. When you meet someone, you more or less intuitively know if that person likes or dislikes you. You don't need to be told. Or, think about a job interview you may have had. Chances are, you immediately liked or disliked the interviewer. Similarly, the interviewer was able to immediately intuit whether you were confident or not. He or she didn't have to be told.

We all have intuitive experiences, but since we tend to value thinking over sensing and feeling, most of us haven't had much practice in using our intuition. Furthermore, our conformist society doesn't encourage us to listen to our inner voice.

However, among the three elements of our Career Compass, intuition is probably the most important since it is also the scanner of experience and in-

telligence and has imbedded in it all of the information of past time. Allan Sandage, Astronomer, in the
PBS Program, *The Creation of the Universe*, made
the comment: "Every single atom in your body was
once inside a star." In that sense, we're all related. So,
our intuition has at its command all of the information about life since its beginning—long before Earth
was formed.

Career Compassing and the Lifecareer Ethic

As noted earlier, Career Compassing is doing
what feels right; but it's not done without regard for
others. For example, from time to time I'm asked,
"What if I'm following my Career Compass and I feel
like doing something destructive? Is that okay?"
Absolutely not. Lifecareer has an ethic that's important to know as you think about Career Compassing.
Furthermore, Lifecareer is an idea for the healthy
personality.

Recently, I spent a summer teaching at Loyola
College. While there, I had an opportunity to talk
with Professor Beatrice Sarlos about the Lifecareer
ethic. Her ideas are reflected in the following para-
graphs.

The Lifecareer Ethic

The Lifecareer ethic is an unbroken wholeness.
Its goal is the gradual unfoldment of life, rather than
revolutionary change. Lifecareer creates no rupture
in reality, but is rather a steadily-changing continu-
ity. A religious system, for example, holds that certain things should be done and that other things
should not be done in accordance with its teachings
regarding *good* and *evil*. But in Lifecareer, anything
that promotes the steady and continuous connection
between one's mental, emotional, physical, and spiri-

tual being is encouraged. Lifecareering supports harmonious development in these four areas.

The ethical obligation of Lifecareer is to take action when anything in life threatens to disrupt this continuous flow. But *flow* as used here, doesn't mean total submission to natural law—nor the '60s idea of *going with the flow*. Rather it means actively participating in one's own development. It's also personal reflection with a special sensitivity—getting new organizations of personal experience and coming up with wholistic impressions.

Further, Lifecareer contains no element of violence. It is the development of the human being at peace with his or herself. Lifecareer does not have to be earned; it is freely available to everyone on Earth. Life is. In Lifecareer unfolding, one exercises responsible stewardship. The reason for this is that you can't own Life: you can only use it. In Lifecareer, you can control your knowledge of and sensitivity to Life, provided you understand that Life doesn't belong to you nor to anyone. Responsible stewardship by each of us means letting our life unfold, naturally in its own unique way.

Living the Lifecareer ethic requires focusing some diligent reflection on where our lives are going and on the information that we are receiving. We begin by asking, "What has gone on before in my life and what is its direction now?" Based on our own inner answers to these questions, we become able to cooperate and flow with Life rather than trying to control it. This can be done without interfering with the career development of others around us. Lifecareer is not career development in the selfish, planned, or traditional sense, it is career development based on deeper knowledge of self.

Lifecareer also is following life in a more positive, non-intrusive way. One doesn't rupture the stream of Life: one *is* the stream. Success requires learning to stream well, divining direction, staying continually active and alert to the movement of the current.

Valuing One's Own Career Compass: A Matter of Cultural Shift and Personal Development

Look at the difficulty of reading and following your Career Compass readings from the standpoint of personal development in our society today. Is it possible that our personal development has followed the major cultural shifts and that events today are forcing us to advance our personal development while also shifting to a new era?

When I talk about *personal development*, I mean a gradual accumulation of understandings that give us a broader view of our life and its relationship to the lives of others. Jane Loevinger's model of Ego (Character) Development as set forth below was helpful to me in gaining those understandings. Loevinger suggests that people go through the following stages or levels:

Impulsive —tends to see the world as good, bad; mean, nice; and clean, dirty.

Self-Protective —tends to blame other people as well as suggest that one should be with the right people and avoid the wrong ones.

Conformist —tends to think about what ought to happen; conventional norms accepted without question.

Self-Aware —sees multiple possibilities, exceptions, and alternatives in situations.

Some people tend to think personal development is a kind of airy fairy idea or abstraction that really doesn't matter in life. However, personal development determines much of our life direction. Why? When you lose your job, for example, the more personal development you have achieved, the more easily you can "pick yourself up, dust yourself off and start all over again." You'll be less inclined to go off the deep end or grow deeply depressed. Personal development also helps marriages hold together. Imagine living with a self-protective type of person or a conformist. The self-protective person is continually blaming the partner for his or her problems. The conformist wants things done according to how they've always been done and any veering away from that can cause conflict. So personal development isn't only something that would be good to have; it's something that's essential in our daily lives because it can reduce stress and give us a better quality of life.

The Agricultural Era and Self-Protection

Now, think about the three major cultural shifts in our society: (1) agricultural; (2) industrial; and (3) postindustrial. Then let's align these cultural shifts with Jane Loevinger's levels of development.

Possible Links of Cultural Shifts with Personal Development	
Agricultural Era	Self-Protection
Industrial Era	Conformity
Postindustrial Era	Self-Awareness

Let's assume that, during the *agricultural era*, society as a whole was functioning at the impulsive and self-protective levels. That is, people were chiefly concerned with survival, with protecting their homes, their land, and their families. In doing so, they blamed most misfortunes which came their way on external causes which in some cases may have been true, but in other cases was not true. At the self-protective level of behavior, people don't tend to see other options or other ways of being. Instead, they usually tend to believe they are victims of circumstance.

The Industrial Era and Conformity

Then, society experienced a cultural jolt and great numbers of people moved from the land to the factory. This was called our industrial period—a time of mass duplication and conformity. This is probably the period in which life planning became systematized much like product planning. Everyone tended to conform, so it no longer seemed obvious that life planning was in many ways different from product planning. The two were just lumped together.

The conformist level of personal development was a perfect fit for the industrial period in which mass production, duplication, and copying were the name of the game. At this point, people were still very busy trying to survive and conformity made them feel more secure. Therefore, few questioned it.

The industrial period and this conformist behavior also fit the popular scientific model of the day which, at that time, had been around for about 300 years. This model held that the parts were equal to the whole, and when put together in a conforming way, these parts would function more efficiently. This notion influenced the career development field as well. Career counselors had their parts (resumes, job search strategies, occupational theories, and the like) that they proposed made the whole. So, lock-step thought and conformity made the industrial period a fairly rigid one. At work, people operated on the corporate compass with few questions asked.

This isn't surprising when we realize that people at the conformist level of development tend to obey rules because they are group accepted rules, not because they fear punishment. These people generally see life as right and wrong, not as right and left. They usually try to do things right, instead of do right things for themselves. Therefore, they don't tend to see life as a whole fabric. They also don't recognize the value of a so-called wrong turn because their perceptions aren't broad enough. Furthermore, they find it difficult to tolerate differences.

It's easy to see how conformity took hold so quickly. At work, people were told what to do. The order of the day was steady work, decent pay, opportunities for advancement, vacation time, and fringe benefits—all supplied by the employer if the employees conformed to the rules. It wasn't necessary to learn many new skills or to read one's Career Compass, as the employer gave the orders and the readings came from the big corporate compass. It was a conformist period, and it worked for both the employer and employee.

The Postindustrial Era and Self-Awareness

Then another jolt shook society and it still is—the movement out of the industrial period into the postindustrial period or information age. Much of what we had learned and conformed to in the industrial era suddenly became obsolete. So, there we were, without information or guidelines, looking around for ways to conform and get into the flow again. But, we didn't find much.

We discovered that this information age calls for a good deal of new learnings that we didn't know we would need. Learning about livelihood getting and maintaining. Many ideas our parents passed down to us are no longer working. Skills we thought would be useful for a lifetime are now either obsolete or rapidly becoming that way. Making ends meet is becoming ever more difficult. Many people who for years had secure jobs are now unemployed and some are homeless. Some are working, but can't afford shelter. A large number of families also are now part of the homeless group. So, we're currently in the *tumble cycle* of life's reorganizations, which is somewhat confusing, even to thousands of folks who thought they had it *made*.

This dramatic and deepening postindustrial shift has had a double effect: (1) we're developing skills we never knew we had; and (2) many people are now living at a lower economic level than they ever dreamed of. All this is offering us the opportunity to grow beyond the conformist level of personal development.

One of the things that has now come clearly into view is the self-aware level of personal development. It is expanding our horizons. As we peek through the cracks at this self-aware level, we can see that we ourselves are becoming aware of being aware. Now that's a major jump in itself. We also see there are many ways of looking at the world, that we no longer have to conform. This means we don't all have to be alike; we can start to see and appreciate our individual differences. At first, this may be both scary and exciting, as it isn't easy to take the first steps, especially when we've been in the habit of conforming and have had definite views about how people should be and not be. But, our excitement mounts as we see that each of us has a Career Compass of our own. Hooray, we don't have to use someone else's!

We step back and catch our breath and stand there in wonderment. Then we realize that all of this has a learning curve, like so much of today's technology. That is, it's going to take time, persistence, risk, and practice.

This vitally needed change in thinking is similar to the one brought about by the voyages of Christopher Columbus. In the 15th Century, most people believed the Earth was flat. They feared that Columbus, in sailing out to sea, would reach the edge of the Earth and fall off. However, Columbus, along with certain learned persons of his time, believed the Earth was round. Therefore, he was confident he would reach his destination. While it took him eight years to gain the needed funding for his expedition, Queen Isabella of Spain eventually agreed to finance it. Columbus set out, intending to forge a new trade route to the Orient by sailing west. Instead, he reached the shores of the New World and opened a whole new continent for exploration. One important outcome was the change in mass perspective that his voyage had brought about: that the Earth was round.

The Earth had always been round, but most people previously had no way to discover or confirm this. Similarly, many people today are unaware that Life, not job, is their career, as social and economic conditions have not been right to help them discover this. When Life-Is-Career, the conditions are also right to move on to the higher levels of self development by reading our individual compasses more and more frequently. This higher level of development can open a whole *new world* to us, ready to be explored—a world that holds as much promise as the one found five centuries ago by Columbus.

Your Question

Are you willing, or are you already making the *journey without distance* back to your own knowing?

16

THE LIFECAREER SKILLS

Differences

Traditional career emphasizes work skills; Lifecareer life skills.

Advancing your Life-as-Career while reading your Career Compass can require the following skills: (1) Organization; (2) Research; (3) Review; (4) Confidence; (5) Faith; (6) Persistence; and (7) Risk Taking. The first three skills are related more to doing things, like organizing your day, researching to improve quality of life (for instance, buying a new item, starting new projects, getting more education, etc.), and reviewing how your decisions are working. The last four skills support the first three and provide the motivation to keep you reading your own Career Compass. These skills were selected because they can keep you active, hopeful, and energetic. They are also necessary to support you as you learn to deliberately

Lifecareer, which may mean you will move from the conforming level to the self-aware level (being who you really are). This simply means you become more individual; you don't follow the crowd. As you start the experience of breaking into your own thought, you will understand the necessity for the skills I have selected.

These skills may at first seem invisible but they can give you visible results. "How do I know I have them if I can't see them?" You can't see life, yet you know it's there. You can't see the wind, yet you know it exists. Or love—you can't see it, but you can certainly feel it. What about music? You can't see it, yet you can thrill to its sounds. Invisible Lifecareer skills are much the same. If you attune yourself to them, learning to see and feel their effects, you will discover how powerfully they can work for you.

These invisible Lifecareer skills won't materialize before your eyes, but they can bring you many tangible results. So let's take a look at some of these skills and attributes—and how to apply them.

Organization

Organization is essential to a smooth-running life. Webster defines *organize* as "to arrange or form into a unity." To each of us, unity has a different meaning.

My husband, David, for example, is a clean desktop person, while I have a desktop filled with papers. I usually have six projects underway simultaneously, while David has two or three, all reasonably organized. Neither is a better system. Each works well for its user. Every system also has some sort of unity, reflecting the sum of the user's approach to work and to life.

If a particular form of organization works well for you, stick with it. Don't try to model your style of organization after someone else's, unless it feels right to you. However, it's helpful to learn how someone else organizes. In the bibliography you'll find a list of books on organization. Some of them may be helpful or none of them may help, but they will provide a start toward learning more about organization.

Research

When I talk about research I don't mean the kind done in academia. Many people think that research only happens in laboratories and college classrooms, but that's just not so. Academic research is only one kind of research.

Personal research is another kind and that's what I'm talking about here. First, there's nothing magical about research. We all do it periodically. Webster defines *research* as a "careful or diligent search." Sometimes our search is for a better price, sometimes quality, sometimes it's in regard to our health, and sometimes education. The quality and accuracy of our information tends to improve our choices.

In some areas, there are so many choices that the occupation of *broker* is appearing more frequently. For instance, we've always had real estate and stock brokers, but now car, telephone, insurance, and printing brokers are becoming more numerous. These people collect the information and sell it to those who don't have time to do it.

Why do I think research is important? Because your decisions are based on your information, and if you listen to what *they* say is correct information, then you may close down many possibilities. For instance, a client who is considering a particular job talks with a counselor about it. She says, "I really would like to work as a paralegal, but my friend says there's no money in it, it's dull and boring work, and there's no possibility for advancement." The counselor suggested she do some research about it:

talk with the schools and to other people in the field
as well as with attorneys. She did and, as a result,
signed up for the program and is very happy. However, had she not done her own research, she would
have passed by this opportunity.

On the other hand, her research could have
influenced her decision in the other direction. But
without her own research, she might still be floun-
dering.

Let's look at research another way. Suppose you
are standing in a line of fifty people in a post office.
You have a yellow slip to pick up a package. To your
right is a window marked "Box mail pickup only."
Would this be a time to do research? No, if you believe everything you read, and yes, if you're into research. The person who had this experience was into
research. He seldom believes what people tell him. So
he stepped to the window and asked the clerk if he
could trade his yellow slip for his package. She said
"Yes." His research paid off.

---

*Minds don't change nearly as fast as
rules and policies.*

Let's look at research from the perspective of
what counselors or teachers tell you. It is probably
the case that most of the advice and opinion passed
along by most counselors or teachers is gained
through reading, through conversation with colleagues, through conferences, and seldom through
direct experience. It is, therefore, important to research your own facts. Don't take someone else's
word for it, as time changes everything. What may
have been the case one week, may not be true the
next. Minds don't change nearly as fast as rules and
policies.

Career Compass Research

Another kind of research is that which we do with our internal data that comes from our experience, intelligence, and intuition. For instance, when we do presentations, whether it's convincing a mate to buy a particular idea or making a presentation to our work staff, our Career Compass is hard at work scanning all the incoming data. We're researching how we like doing whatever we're doing. We're gathering information. When we attend conferences, we're engaged in researching how we feel about the experience, how we like the networking, is it working for us, and if not, why not? We're also gathering information of interest while we're at the conference. So considerable research happens even when we're not aware of it.

As we live with mates and friends, we're constantly reviewing and researching that experience asking ourselves important questions about how it's working. Sometimes we act on that information, sometimes we don't.

Research is important to our Lifecareer both economically and personally. Research becomes particularly important when you stop using someone else's Career Compass readings, because this means you're finding out for youself; you are getting updated current information.

Review

Review is a very important skill, again linked to your Career Compass. As you commit more to your own journey, you need more time for review. For instance, you have ideas, you try a few of them, and you wait to see the result. Then you review. Review is a daily activity in Career Compassing.

Review is also important in regard to health and diet because we tend to forget. Our weight increases by one pound, then two, and before we know it, we have an additional five pounds that we're going to do something about tomorrow. But tomorrow seldom comes and good intentions wane. That's what review is all about. If we mark our calendar for a regular review, then we have a better chance of reminding ourselves about the situation and then doing something about it.

Most of my review information comes to me during my quiet times when I deliberately listen to my Career Compass. To add structure to my review, I have notebooks for each of my review areas. If it's a frequently used area I use a three-ring notebook; if it's a smaller area, I use a spiral notebook. I find tracking and documenting my thought very useful. Buckminister Fuller kept what he called a *Chronofile* and when he died he had box upon box of notes. I don't get quite that detailed about it, but each person is different. Some of my clients document their thought in their personal journals with notation statements, others write short poems. However, if you have an intention of reviewing and keeping track of your thought, the right structure will come to you.

Confidence

Contrary to popular belief, confidence is not something we either have or don't have—rather, it's a skill we can develop.

Start by saying aloud, "I am a powerful and wonderful person." Say it regularly. Say it to your reflection in the mirror. Say it as you drive or while taking a stroll or preparing meals. Say it with conviction—don't merely say it, feel it. You may be surprised at the changes you'll observe in yourself as you start to know it experientially, not merely in your head. After all, it's true. It's time you started to know it. And you can—just by replacing your harsh, overly critical attitude toward yourself with this good, positive, healthy confidence-builder.

As we have seen, everything is connected. If we are fearful, our confidence in ourselves and in our ability to act is reduced. Furthermore, if we don't feel confidence, we can't communicate it. People instinctively know this. They can read us by our thoughts, words, and gestures. And we know instantly how someone else feels about us—he or she doesn't have to tell us verbally. The information we receive through our feelings (the electromagnetic band) is powerful and accurate. It transmits directly to the people with whom we come in contact. Thus, if we are not confident, our interviewer, boss, mate, friends, even strangers know it immediately.

Recent crime research, in fact, indicates that, if you walk in a fearful, uncertain way, you are more likely to be mugged than if you walk confidently. Your uncertainty shows in your body movements. This may be reason enough to work on building your confidence.

Think about the poised, confident people you know. What makes them so forceful, so self-assured? Consider it. You may learn a lot.

And realize that what you feel inside communicates to everyone around you. We transmit our feeling about ourselves in our eyes, our words, our tone of voice, our gestures, our very being. We are our thoughts. So if we don't like what we are, we must change what we believe about ourselves. That will change us—and change what we communicate to others.

Faith

For many, faith is a little-used invisible skill, lying dormant within. Modern usage has largely assigned faith to the realm of religion, linking it to belief in God. However, I use faith to mean how deeply you believe in what you are and in your ability to be who you are. According to Webster, *faith* is "firm belief in something for which there is no proof; complete confidence, and something that is believed with strong conviction."

Faith, in your purpose, your life path, and your intelligence, enriches your Life-as-Career. If you have faith, feel it, and live it, your Lifecareer will unfold for you—in some very surprising ways.

You don't have to push life, prod it, or wait for it. It simply unfolds because you have faith and act upon it. It's what helps you to continue trusting your Career Compass. Faith is pure, unquestioning belief in something for which no tangible proof exists. Intuition is your mind knowing. Faith is your soul knowing.

I once asked Buckminster Fuller if he believed that the universe would support him as long as he was doing work that was meaningful to society and humanity. He replied, "No, I don't believe it, I have utter faith in it. I have a 53-year success experiment." The reason Fuller changed the word from *belief* to *faith* is that he defined a belief as "a hand-me-down claim to 'reality' personally untested and potentially unfounded (versus knowing)."

Fuller, after all, didn't talk about faith. He lived it. He knew that faith is like a muscle—the more you use it, the stronger it becomes and the more work it will do.

Persistence

Persistence is important as a support to your Career Compass. It's one of the most valuable skills. It can help determine whether and how you'll make it, whether on your own terms or someone else's. You probably recall the emphasis placed in school on being persistent and dependable. How persistent you are is largely related to what rewards you may get as a result of being so. Such rewards can be either inter-

nal or external. For example, you can work for what
someone else pays you—or for your own gratifica-
tion and fulfillment. Most work yields some of both of
these types of rewards.

It is interesting to read about people who have
made it. Most of these people didn't *make it* on other
people's terms, but they did succeed in doing so on
their own. One common theme running through
most of these accounts is their persistent belief that
they could make it coupled with their persistent effort
to do just that, regardless of what anyone else said or
thought.

I recall reading about the resistance that author
Richard Bach encountered, for example, in trying to
sell his simple manuscript about a sea gull. He netted
rejection slips from many publishers before one at
last said that *Jonathan Livingston Seagull* had merit.
Had Bach simply given up, the manuscript would
now be gathering dust and his writing career would
not have bloomed as it has. However, he persisted,
and his work was published.

As you can see, all of these invisible skills are
connected. To be persistent, you must have faith and
confidence, and these, in turn, are built upon a well-
developed awareness. You might say that persistence
is hope. Not as in, "I hope I make it." Hope in the persistent sense is closely related to faith. Hope is a feeling that springs from deep within—a persistent feeling that helps you to maintain your faith and confidence while you work for what you want.

Those who do not have persistence lack what is
called staying power. Large numbers of very tal-
ented people fall out of the race because, for one reason or another, they just didn't persist. They did not
believe. Or worse, they believed it when someone else
told them, "You really don't have it." They allowed
another's assessment of their ability and potential to
override their own. Mark Twain said, "We are handi-

capped only by what we think we cannot do." We are also handicapped by believing what others say we cannot do.

Persistence, then, is faith in action. It is believing that we can reach our goal. It is also the ability to keep working toward it, even though we may have no proof that we will achieve it.

We know inside that doing so is correct. And doing so when we receive little or no support from others requires twice the amount of confidence and faith. We cannot be as persistent if we do not feel good and right about what we are pursuing. Belief in self and reliance on intuition are essential to persisting—and achieving. Theodore Roosevelt put it this way:

> The credit belongs to the man (woman) who is actually in the arena, whose face is marred by dust and sweat and blood, who knows the great enthusiasm, the great devotion, and spends himself (herself) in a worthy cause; who, if (s)he wins, knows the thrills of high achievement, and who, if (s)he fails, at least fails while daring greatly, so that his (her) place shall never be with those cold and timid souls who know neither victory nor defeat.
> (Parentheses added)

Don't be misled into thinking that persistence is something one is born with—that either you have it or you don't. Persistence can be learned and developed through practice. When you want something badly enough, you can learn very quickly how to persist.

If you're working toward something you want and know is right, you may be walking that road alone. You even may have to pursue a less-traveled road or trail blaze one of your own. Don't be discouraged by it. As Robert Frost observed:

> "Two roads diverged in a wood, and I...,
> I took the one less traveled by,
> And that has made all the difference."

Risk Taking

Another Lifecareer skill is taking risks. If you are serious about advancing your Lifecareer by reading your Career Compass, you will find risk taking a necessary skill. Many people shy away from this thrilling, challenging skill. Sure, it's scary to take a risk, but it's an interesting way to get from here to there. It's also one way to try out your dreams and ideas. Life is too short to always play it safe. *Safe* holds you down, makes you stale.

Playing it safe is only an illusion anyway. We think we're playing it safe, but what we probably are doing is avoiding what's going on around us, and that may be the biggest risk of all. By not acting, we are reacting. We are being done to rather than doing. This brings to mind former Idaho Senator Frank Church, who died in April, 1984 at the age of 59. At 23, Church had been told he had cancer. The doctors said he had only six months to live. Church was to live another 36 years. Discussing how his illness had reshaped his outlook, Church said:

> I had previously tended to be more cautious. But having so close a brush with death at 23, I felt afterwards that life itself is such a chancy proposition that the only way to live it is by taking great chances.

It's amazing how many risks turn into successful adventures (that others later enviously regard as safe, conservative ventures). It's probably equally amazing how many successful adventures eventu-

ally fold. That's due in part to the universal law of
dissipative structures. As you recall, this holds that
the more fixed and stable something becomes, the
greater its potential for instability. Or, when you
think everything is set, look out for change.

Creating one's future is risky, but it's even more
risky to allow someone else to create it for you. At
least, when you create it, it's yours. You know what it
is, and though it may not work out exactly as you
hoped, you can gain a fortune in learning and understanding. Risking is acknowledging you're alive.

Free Yourself from
What Others Think

Finally, one of the most needed and least used
invisible Lifecareer skills is *freeing yourself from
what others think*. It's difficult because people may
label you *closed*. That is, they may be critical of you
because they think you're missing important information. However it's important to be choiceful about
when you want to receive information from others.
Why? For two reasons, (1) when others give you information from their Career Compass, you will probably have to think about what you received. This
takes time you could spend carrying out what you
have heard from your own Career Compass; and
(2) unsolicited feedback could cause you to doubt
your own Career Compass information and you may
abandon your own understandings.

To free yourself from others' unsolicited thought
is somewhat difficult. So, it's important to develop
some skills in fending off unwanted feedback. One
good way to avoid unsolicited feedback is don't bring
up or discuss your life direction or any other concern
you have, until you are sure you have the strength to
go ahead with what you were initially thinking. If the
topic comes up, just don't comment.

For instance, Nancy was with a group of people

who were determined to advise her on a particular
problem. She tried to politely avoid their comments.
Finally, one of them said, "You don't really want my
feedback, do you?" She replied, "No," and that was
the end of the conversation. It wasn't easy for her to
say "No," but it was important to protect her own
thought until she decided to ask for information. Her
strategy, therefore, is to not bring up topics she
doesn't want feedback about, and if they are brought
up by someone else, she extinguishes the comments
by little or no reply. She doesn't choose to use her
time on argument or debate. She decides when she
wants to receive feedback. Each of us needs to figure
out our own strategy. What works for one person
may be a disaster with another one. However, becoming aware of and using our right to be choiceful
is something we can all do.

As we learn how to use our Career Compasses,
we will see that we are the new explorers, navigating
in much the same way as Columbus did—by relying
on experience, intelligence, and intuition—only this
time sailing inward, searching for our own truth. By
so doing, we can began to live life on our own terms.

How does one learn to read his or her Career
Compass? By doing it regularly—and continually,
despite any feelings of self doubt. David Reynolds, in
his book *Playing Ball on Running Water*, writes of a
young prince, who at a very early age, was suddenly
faced with becoming king, owing to his father's serious illness. The prospect caused the young prince to
panic. He told everyone he wasn't ready. He thought,
if his mother were alive, she could assume the throne.
Then he wondered why his sisters couldn't.

Two days before the coronation, the young
prince suddenly locked himself in his room. He refused to come out. The ailing king summoned the
grand wizard to his bedside and told him to solve the
problem.

That night at suppertime, the grand wizard knocked on the prince's door. He was told to go away. However, the wizard persisted. "I have a dynastic pill for you to take with your meal," he said. "You cannot reign without taking this dynastic pill."

The prince said that he had never heard of such a thing. The grand wizard ignored the comment and told him where the bottle containing the pill was located. He advised him to read the instructions carefully before taking it.

The prince found the bottle. He picked it up and read the label. It said, *Dynastic Pill*. The label indicated that the pill was personally prepared by each monarch for his royal successor. The prince opened the bottle and saw the piece of paper bearing the instructions. As he began to read them, he suddenly started to daydream about the coronation banquet. He could see himself standing regally at the head table, toasting the people of his kingdom.

Two days later, the royal coronation took place. All who attended talked about the splendid bearing of the young king. They speculated he would be another in a long line of wise monarchs.

After the excitement of the day had died down, the prince, now a king, returned to his chamber to finish reading the note he had found in the bottle. It said:

For you, my son.

> No man is ever ready for such authority as this. No man begins by feeling like a king. You become a king by being one. In time, you will wear your crown as comfortably as anyone has. There is no magic in the pill. It is made of the bitterest herbs. The instructions are to hold it in your mouth until you grow used to the bitterness. Then, when you

have conquered it, when the pill has completely dissolved, you may swallow it. That's all.

Your loving father (p. 137)

When we can similarly overcome the bitter taste of self-doubt, and continue to be guided by our own Career Compass (our own experience, intelligence, and intuition), we will be rewarded with confidence and growth. As Brian Swimme said in *The Universe Is a Green Dragon*, "If you surprise the world with your life, the world will surprise you at death."

17

AFTER ALL IS SAID AND DONE

Differences

Traditional career focuses mostly on the individual life;
Lifecareer acknowledges the connectedness
of each life to all lives.

All of our destinies are much more interconnected than we may realize. And they have far more
impact on one another—and on the whole—than we
conceive. Some people, for example, pop out of the
space-time continuum bent on making a big splash
only to wind up creating but a small ripple. Yet,
while it seems small, like a wave created by a pebble
dropped in a pond, it may reach to the farthest
shores, touching all. So a seemingly small ripple may
exert as much impact, in the long run, as the far-
thest-reaching wave. And over time, it blends into
and becomes part of the whole we are all co-creating
in our individual ways. Conversely, other people
don't contemplate anything out of the ordinary, yet
end up making a big splash.

Over the years, I have frequently heard it said, "Each job is important." And I agree—it is. But, at first, I thought this was an effort to try to console those who work at lower-paying jobs. Now, I realize it is much more significant than that. Each job that any of us works at, at any time in life, serves a purpose. Yes, it benefits us, but it benefits others, too—our destinies are linked in very intricate and subtle ways. Each job is a learning experience, and each learning is contributing to the evolution of the world. We may not realize it, but that's what we are doing. In fact, what we think we are doing—and what evolution is actually doing—may be quite different.

Consider the widely-publicized case of Karen Ann Quinlan. At 21, Karen attended a party, where she apparently had several alcoholic drinks. These, combined with a mild tranquilizer she is thought to have ingested with them, reportedly caused her to lapse into a coma. She never regained consciousness. In a historic right-to-die case, Karen's parents petitioned the court to order the removal of the respirator that was helping to keep her alive. The New Jersey Supreme Court, in a 1976 landmark ruling, declared that Karen could be removed from the respirator. She died nine years later, while still in a coma, on June 11, 1985. A tragic story? Perhaps. Yet Karen's parents feel that her life still serves a purpose: it led them to found the Karen Ann Quinlan Center for Hope, which provides hospice care for the terminally ill.

Each life, then, has meaning. And each unfolds in a distinct way. Sometimes we are in the role of teaching others, and sometimes, they are teaching us. Who we are individually probably doesn't matter much in the long run except to us. As we each come and go and make our contributions and leave our piece of history, we begin to realize we *are* the world—we are each pieces of the *whole,* struggling to know what it means to be fully human. Some of us get quick flashes of what that may be like. Others simply focus on their jobs and their personal lives as being all there is. Striving to know what it is like to be *fully human* means seeking to gain a clearer picture of how intimately all of our lives are interwoven. One person dies, but from that life comes contributions that benefit countless others. Another person loses his or her job and, from that, learns much about priorities and survival.

Jean, for example, quit her teaching job of 15 years to have children and raise a family. She now understands what it means to struggle financially. Even so, she has a greater appreciation of what she has. Jean feels she is touching the lives of her two sons in very special ways. And who knows what they will contribute to the evolutionary pattern as a result.

Jean has a wealthy grandmother who could make life fairly easy for her. But the grandmother does not choose to do so. It is hard for Jean to understand, but it's meant to be that way for a reason that is bigger than she or her grandmother can see.

In contrast, another woman felt a strong need to pursue her growth and development in a different way. She got a job and gave over the care of her children to a housekeeper. She worried about being gone from her children. But, from this experience, her children now say they learned how to follow their destinies. They also will be more able to love and nurture their own children while working outside the home if it becomes important for them to do so.

Still another example is James. He had a Ph.D. and lived in a large city, but could not find a suitable job there. The only job offer he received was one from a company in another state. He accepted the offer and moved to that state. James loves both the job and his new locale. Finding a job in his hometown just was not meant to be.

These are but three examples of connectedness and the realization that some things are meant to be, in spite of all the discussion about how things *ought to be*. There is no one way to live life, for each life is intricately linked with many other lives, and with its own destiny.

For these reasons, life often has a very different purpose for us than we have. And when things don't work out as we want, that may be life giving us a signal about our individual destiny. Each of us knows someone, for example, who does not have impressive work qualities, and yet, for some reason, lands a choice job or a handsome promotion. Then there are those persons who know little about business, yet are able to launch their own firms and achieve financial success. And all of us know people who have done things we thought impossible or who have fallen into spectacular good fortune. What life does and what we expect it to do are often quite different.

John, for example, was scheduled to be on Flight 290 out of Chicago on May 24th. A last-minute business meeting forced him to cancel his reservation. Soon after Flight 290 took off that day, the plane suddenly began to lose altitude. Moments later, it plunged to the ground and burst into flames. There were no survivors. John wasn't meant to be on that flight. His work was not yet finished.

Then there is Cleo, who recently obtained her Ph.D. after years of study and started to do some very original and important research. Then she discovered that she had terminal cancer. She realized her life was coming to an end. "Like a rosebud," she says, "my life was just beginning to open and bloom, and now the petals are suddenly dropping."

Another example is Sally, who, after graduating from college *suma cum laude,* went to work for a Boston insurance company where her friend Jan

was employed. Jan had dropped out of college at the
end of her sophomore year and after just two years
with the firm advanced to the level of vice president.
Sally has now been with the firm for over two years
and still has a rank-and-file job. Having more academic background than Jan, she wonders why she
has not been similarly promoted to a key position.

In contrast, Brad earned a degree in business
management and after graduation, got a job chauf-
feuring a limousine. "Why don't you get a job in
management?" his mother asks.

"It doesn't feel right," says Brad. "And I like what
I'm doing now. It's interesting—and I meet some ter-
rific people."

His mother doesn't understand this. "After we
spent so much money putting him through college,"
she despairs, "why does he want to drive a limousine?" There are no simple answers—only patterns
that emerge over the long term to reveal the reasons
why.

Many people, for example, have what it takes to
do very responsible jobs. Yet when they try to obtain
such jobs, they repeatedly run into roadblocks. "You
can do it," people tell them. "Just try again. And give
it your best." They do. But it just doesn't work.

The result is that people like these tend to carry
around stress and disappointment most of their lives
rather than realize that the *great job* they sought just
wasn't in the cards for them. Or as Dr. Paul Brenner
would say, "...some people just come out of the Bingo
Shoot at the right time." If we looked at the pattern of
life from a higher perspective, we would realize that
each of us is *doing all we know how to do.* In other
words, given our physiological, intellectual, and psychological capacities, and the day, time, situation,
and people involved, we are performing *the best we
know how.*

So, after all is said and done, as you review the

limitless choices in life, thinking you may have missed out on your career, know that you haven't. *Life* is career. And, as the new science confirms, we are all self-organizing systems that keep on keeping on. Therefore, we don't have to *find our way* before we let go; we can trust the process using our Career Compass.

As we journey forward, we know that our body particles are intelligent and that they somehow managed to construct us without outside help into superb human becomings. Along the way, society may make it more difficult for us to become, but even that can be useful to us as we learn what it means to be more fully human. As we do, we come to realize that we are the generation chosen to live at this monumental turning point in human history—the beginning of the Universal Age, an age in which success means making it *on our own terms*.

> We are one body, one universal species, born into this universe at the dawn of the Universal Age. The vision of the future affirms the visions of the past. We have always known we are one body, now we see we are. We have always believed we are immortal, and now we see that the human race, indeed is infinite. We have always felt that we will contact higher being, and now we see that we, ourselves, are higher beings. The commandment of the Universal Age is to know more of God, to know more of the patterns of evolution. As infinitesimal co-creators, we greet the Universe with the awareness that we are one, we are whole, we are good, we are universal. ***Earthbound history has ended. Universal history has begun.*** The meaning of our crisis is to activate our new potential, and the purpose of our power is universal life; and we knew it all the time.
>
> Barbara Marx Hubbard

APPENDIX A

Why Lifecareer?

Growing up as I did in West Virginia, I learned about life, survival, relationships, love, hot chocolate chip cookies, lemon meringue pies, licking cake dough bowls, raising a garden, sewing, attending school, going to church, and more—all of these things were life to me. I was growing and learning. No one bothered me about career. In fact, one of my greatest blessings was not having a school counselor, prodding me to choose a career.

Nor did my family urge me to settle on a career. Instead, they suggested I develop a marketable skill of some sort, so, if times grew hard, I could survive. That proved to be a good idea. However, my family allowed me to find that skill in my own time. That was another blessing.

As I grew up, life seemed whole to me. Career was an abstract notion. I may have heard the word two or three times, but it didn't mean much. Why? Because Life was career to me. All parts of it worked—not always the way I wanted it to—but it worked. Often much better than I had planned. And there didn't seem to be much need to structure it.

I graduated from high school without having a marketable skill. To gain experience, I went to work in a department store. There, I learned that I wanted to develop a skill that would give me more options than working behind a counter. Thus, with the help of my parents, I decided to earn an Associate of Arts degree in Business Administration. I started the course and a year later dropped out. By this time, I had very good secretarial skills. I continued working and took evening classes each semester to have something interesting to do. After nine years, I looked at my transcript and discovered that I probably had enough units to graduate with a four-year degree in Business Administration if I wanted to. So I did.

I continued taking night classes while working and soon discovered that I had enough units to obtain a Master's Degree.

Soon after earning my M.A., I decided that I wanted to write. I thought I would need a Ph.D. to be considered knowledgeable. (Only later did I learn that knowledge—not degrees—makes one knowledgeable.) Meanwhile, the company I was working for merged with another company, and I was fortunate to be in a position to receive a pay-off due to my job being abolished. I used this money, along with assistantships and loans, to pay for my Ph.D. program.

In the course of my doctoral studies, I was introduced to career development. Imagine—I had made it all the way to a Ph.D. without knowing anything about career development! Career still remained only an idea to me, not much more. I viewed it as important in my academic program, but not as part of my life. Then, as I began to study career development theories, I realized they were mostly linked to occupation, not to life. So I decided, "I'll study them for my classes, take my tests, and get on with life." And I did that.

But the discrepancies between these academic career theories and what I experienced in life fascinated me. I couldn't stop thinking about them. And my later work as a guidance counselor with middle- and secondary-school students, confirmed that the career theories I had learned in graduate school not only didn't work for me, but didn't work too well for the students, either. The career techniques didn't fare much better, though some of them were useful. As to career decision making, the students thought they did that well. One of them said, "If it doesn't go right, then I will just have to make another choice. And I do that as well as anyone."

At this point, I stopped teaching decision making in order to research it. I wanted to learn more about the process of adolescent decision making. In the meetings that followed with each of my 300 students during each of their four years of high school, I stopped using all formal career programs. I wanted to see what students would do as they followed their own experience, intelligence, and intuition. Added to this, I could observe their decision-making process. I could also encourage and facilitate what they felt were their next steps in life. I cared more about their next steps than about their long-term goals. I also trusted their intelligence and their life experience. If life didn't go right for them, I knew it would go left, and therein would be the learning. Besides, as I looked around I saw that most adults also were learning from misdirections.

Added to this, I knew that attitudes affected the body and health. In my reading, I had discovered that a strong link exists between time urgency and increase in blood pressure, blood cholesterol, heart and respiratory rate, the blood levels of insulin, and other physical factors. I wanted to work with career in a more holistic way. While I was trying to learn more about the adolescent decision-making process, I wanted to do so in ways gentle to the body.

I soon discovered in talking with the students that enabling and encouraging their next steps, not imposing the past on them, but hearing how it was from their personal reality and validating that reality was a powerful approach. Once again I was reminded of the great discrepancies between what I had learned about career in graduate school and my own experience, both personal and professional. These differences eventually brought about *Lifecareer*.

But why invent *Lifecareer*? What do I have to say that hasn't been said before? First, and most important, I wanted to introduce the idea of a career philosophy. This notion came to me after reading the experiences of Vice Admiral James Bond Stockdale, USN, while a North Vietnam prisoner of war. He said that during his confinement, "the so-called practical academic exercises in how to do things...were useless." He noted that, in stress situations, classical teachings served him best. Admiral Stockdale was particularly influenced by Epictetus' *The Enchiridion*, a manual for Roman field soldiers. One line that he particularly liked and found useful was "Men are not disturbed by things, but by the view they take of things."

Similarly, Viktor Frankl, in *Man's Search for Meaning*, describes the will to survive among concentration-camp prisoners who believed it when they were told they would be released soon. When they were not released, as they expected to be, many of them died. Both Stockdale and Frankl agree that how one perceives a situation is critical to survival.

I then decided that a philosophy of career was needed that would work for us when we feel we are similarly imprisoned in the confines of life. My experience is that while many people know the techniques of the work career—resume writing, job search, occupation information gathering—they don't realize that their career philosophy is directly related to what is happening in their lives.

I also wanted to develop a career philosophy that would convey wholeness—that life and career are one. And I wanted to explain the unfolding of *Lifecareer*, as we unfold a book page by page when we read it. To convey this total concept, I coined the word "Lifecareer." It denotes both life in its totality and the journey through life.

Further, I wanted people to know they are living their careers—now—rather than letting *career* be something they might only one day have.

Too, learning about new physics served to validate my experience of life—that life works, that it is patterned. I wanted to share my understanding of both *Lifecareer* and this new science—and how they support one another. The principles of the new physics convinced me as never before that we are all one—the universe, people, plants, animals. We are all subatomic particles and waves formed in many shapes and sizes and colors. As a young woman of Hopi descent told me recently, "Everything else knows it is part of the universe—only humans have trouble with that idea." This set me to remembering how I had been taught separateness, almost from infancy. I had been told, for example, that the flower grows from the seed. Yet David Bohm, author of *Wholeness and the Implicate Order* observes, "You may think that a plant unfolds from the seed, but it's not just the seed. It must be the whole environment which unfolds into a plant."

The final reasons for my inventing of *Lifecareer* were: (1) to validate the experience of a growing number of people who know that Life-is-career but need support to keep following it; (2) to help those just learning that Life-is-career; and (3) to support the children of the world in living their lives as career.

We are each only different pieces of the large life puzzle. And it's my hope that *Lifecareer* will help you get in closer touch with your unique piece.

APPENDIX B
LIFECAREER FOUNDATION ACTIVITIES
NEED HELP?

This book explains and illustrates the *Lifecareer* approach, yet does not detail how to apply it since each reader's needs and goals are different. As such, they must be worked out personally. But what if you are in transition or considering transition? The answer is simple. Here at *Lifecareer Foundation*, we are always available to counsel you on your lifecareer concerns, in person or by phone. One to three sessions may be all that is necessary to achieve the answers you need to go forward confidently with your life.

If you have lifecareer concerns and would like to discuss them, phone or write us today at the address listed below.

LIFECAREER LEARNING OPPORTUNITIES

College Programs

The *Lifecareer* approach detailed in this book, pioneered by career-development specialists Anna Miller-Tiedeman, Ph.D., and David V. Tiedeman, Ed.D., has been heralded by educators at Johns Hopkins University and other leading institutions.

Its growing endorsement by career counselors nationwide led to the development of the *Lifecareer* graduate and postgraduate studies program now offered at William Lyon University. Further information about these programs can be obtained by writing to the *Lifecareer Foundation*.

Seminars and Workshops

Today, *Lifecareer* guidance and training are available to both the public and career professionals through *Lifecareer Foundation* in formats ranging from seminars and half-day group orientation programs to on-campus workshops and faculty and corporate training programs. All are designed to help those who attend to understand and to apply the new *Lifecareer* perspective.

Consultation to Business and Industry

Expanding on their roles as consultants to universities and colleges, Anna Miller-Tiedeman, Ph.D., and David V. Tiedeman, Ed.D., are now available to consult on the implementation of the *Lifecareer* approach with corporate managers, personnel administrators, and other decision makers in business and industry.

For information about the above programs, write or phone:

Lifecareer Foundation
993 "C" S. Santa Fe Ave #180
Vista, CA 92083
(619) 726-6700

BIBLIOGRAPHY

Bach, R. *Illusions: The adventures of a reluctant messiah.* New York: Dell/Eleanor Friede, 1977.

Bateson, G. *Mind and nature: A missing unity.* New York: Bantam Books, 1979.

Bennis, W. *Interview with Don Gevirtz.* Foothill Group, Beverly Hills, CA. (Videotape). Los Angeles, CA: interview, University of Southern California, 1983.

Bennis, W. *The Tiedeman's Interview Warren Bennis.* Cassette tape, Lifecareer Foundation, 993 "C" S. Santa Fe Av, No. 180, Vista, CA 92083, 1983.

Bennis, W. and Nanus, B. *Leaders: Strategies for taking charge.* New York: Harper and Row, 1985.

Bohm, D. *Wholeness and the implicate order.* Boston: Routledge and E. Paul Kegan, 1980.

Bohm, D. *On freedom and the individual.* Working Papers for the Conference: Physics and the Ultimate Significance of Time, Claremont: Center for Process Studies, 1325 N. College Avenue, 91711, 1982.

Bradbury, R. *Collected poems.* Northridge, CA: Lord Jim Press, 1983.

Bradbury, R. *Inspiration and how to get it.* Keynote Speech, Santa Barbara (CA) Writers Conference, June 18, 1982.

Bradley, D. On board. *Motor Boating and Sailing,* November, 1982, 150 (5).

Braine, J. Starting afresh, *Quest 80,* 1980.

Brenneman, R. J. *Fuller's earth.* New York: St. Martin's Press, 1984.

Bryant-Quinn, J. Comments on career. *Cosmopolitan,* August, 1982.

Bylinsky, G. The race to the automatic factory. *Fortune,* February 21, 1983.

Byrne, J. It takes more than a degree. *Forbes,* December 3, 1984.

Byrne, J. The m.b.a. mills. *Forbes,* December 19, 1984, November 19, 1984.

Campbell, J. *The power of myth.* New York: Doubleday & Co., 1988.

Camus, A. *The myth of sisyphus.* New York: Vintage Books, 1955.

Capra, F. *The turning point: Science, society, and the rising culture.* New York: Simon and Schuster, 1982.

Capra, F. *New science.* Cassette tape. Lifecareer Foundation, 993 "C" S. Santa Fe Av, No. 180, Vista, CA 92083, 1983.

Carroll, L. *Alice in Wonderland.* New York: Pocket Books, 1951.

Cousins, N. *Anatomy of an illness.* New York: Norman, 1979.

Cousins, N. The physician as wordsmith. *Transcript,* Los Angeles: University of Southern California. 2 (32), January 6, 1983.

Cox, J. Discoveries. *Organic Gardening,* November 29 (11), 1982.

Directory of firms operating in foreign countries. New York: Uniworld Inc., 1984.

Dossey, L. *Space, time & medicine.* Boulder and London: Shambhala, 1982.

Federal Deposit Insurance Corporation, Annual Report, Washington, D.C.: 1984.

Fezler, W. *Just imagine: A guide to visualization using imagery.* Hollywood: Gaurida Books Publishing Company, 1980.

Ferguson, M. *The aquarian conspiracy.* Los Angeles: J. P. Tarcher, Inc., 1980.

Frankl, V. *Man's search for meaning.* New York: Pocket Books, 1973.

Frost, R. *Robert Frost's poems*. New York: Pocket Books, 1948.

Fuller, B. *Critical path*. New York: St. Martin's Press, 1981a.

Fuller, B. *Intuition*. New York: Doubleday & Co., 1970.

Fuller, B. Personal conversation with the Tiedeman's. Pacific Palisades, CA: The Fuller residence, January 22, 1981b.

Fuller, B. *Synergetics*. New York: MacMillan Publications, 1975.

Fuller, B. *Tetrascroll: Goldilocks and the three bears*. New York: St. Martin's Press, 1982.

Gawain, S. *Creative visualization*. Mill Valley, CA: Whatever Publishing Co., 1978.

Gibran, K. *The prophet*. New York: Alfred A. Knopf, 1973.

Harrison, R. *Leadership and strategy for a new age. Lessons from "conscious evolution."* Xerox, 1982.

HayGroup. 1988 Environmental scan: People and pay in the '90s. One Landmark Square, Stamford, CT, May 1988.

Haynes, J. *Workers of the world unite and stop working!* Paris: Dandalion Press, 1978.

Higginson, T. W. (Translator) *The enchiridion—Epictetus*. Indianapolis: Bobbs Merrill Educational Publishing Co., 1955.

Hofstadter, D. R. *Gödel, Escher, Bach: an eternal golden braid*. New York: Vintage Books, 1980.

Hubbard, B. M. *The evolutionary journey*. San Francisco: Evolutionary Press, 1982.

Hubbard, B. M. *New being*. Cassette Tape, Lifecareer Foundation, 993 "C" S. Santa Fe Av, No. 180, Vista, CA 92083.

Johnson, R. A. *HE: understanding masculine psychology*. New York: Harper and Row, 1974.

Juhan, D. *Job's body*. Station Barrytown, NY: Station Hill Press, 1987.

Kalmbach, P. et al. Robots effect on production, work and employment. *The Industrial Robot*, 1982.

Keleman, S. *Living your dying*. Berkeley: Center Press, 1974.

Kubler-Ross, E. *On death and dying*. New York: McMillan, 1969.

Loevinger, Jane. *Ego development*. San Francisco: Jossey-Bass, 1970.

Los Angeles Times. Panel says automation brings more jobs, June 18, 1987.

Lukas, M. The world according to Ilya Prigogine. *Quest 80*, 1980.

Maslow, A. H. *Motivation and personality*. New York: Harper, 1954.

McLuhan, M. *The medium is the massage*. New York: Bantam Books 1967.

Murphy, T. P. Do not fold, spindle or mutilate. *Forbes*, November 5, 1984.

Ornstein, R. *The psychology of consciousness*. New York: Viking Penguin Books, 1975.

O'Toole, J. Getting ready for the next industrial revolution. *National Forum, The Phi Kappa Phi Journal*, Winter, 1983.

O'Toole, J. How to forecast your own working future. *The Futurist* (16) 1, February, 1982.

O'Toole, J. Second industrial revolution calls for generalists. *Transcript*, Los Angeles: University of Southern California, November 15, 1982.

Personal glimpses of Bucky Fuller. *The Futurist*. October 1983.

Postman, N. Sunrise semester. Channel 2, Chicago, IL.

Prigogine, I. *From being to becoming: time and complexity in the physical sciences*. San Francisco: W.H. Freeman, 1980.

Reynalds, D. *Playing ball on running water.* New York: Quill, 1984.
Roberts, J. *The individual and the nature of mass events.* Englewood Cliffs, NJ: Prentice-Hall, Inc., 1981.
Rumberger, R. W., Levin, H. M. *Forecasting the impact of new technologies on the future job market* (Project Report No. 84-A4). Palo Alto: Stanford University, Institute for Finance and Governance, 1984.
Sagan, C. *Cosmos.* New York: Random House, 1983.
Sandage, A. *Creation of the universe—notes on physics.* PBS Special, PTV Publications, P.O. Box 701, Kent, OH, 1986.
Santa Barbara Writers Conference. Carpinteria, CA 93015: Mary Conrad, Coordinator, P. O. Box 304, 1982.
Sarlos, B. Personal Conversation. Baltimore, MD: 1987.
Stockdale, Admiral J. B. The world of Epictetus: reflections on survival and leadership. *Atlantic Monthly,* April, 1983.
Strauch, R. *The reality illusion.* Wheaton, Il.: The Theosophical Publishing House, 1983.
Swimme, B. *The universe is a green dragon.* Santa Fe, NM: Bear & Co., Inc., 1984.
The Holy Bible. King James Version.
The right note isn't everything. *Harvard Magazine,* May-June, 1982.
Toffler, A. *The third wave.* New York: William Morrow, 1980.
Toynbee, A. *A study of history.* New York: Oxford University Press, 1972.
Tsu, L. *Tao te ching.* New York: Vintage Books, 1972.
U. S. Congress. Joint Economic Committee. *Estimating the effects of economic change on national health and social well-being. A study prepared for the use of the subcommittee on economic goals and intergovernmental policy,* Washington, D.C.: U. S. Government Printing Office, June 15, 1984.
U. S. Department of Commerce, Bureau of the Census. *Detailed occupation and years of school completed by age, for the civilian labor force by sex, race, and spanish origin.* Washington, D.C.: U.S. Government Printing Office, 1980 Census of Population, March, 1983.
U. S. Department of Commerce, Bureau of the Census. *Statistical abstract of the United States.* Washington, D.C.: U. S. Government Printing Office, 1988.
U. S. Department of Commerce. International Trade Administration. *The Robotics Industry, Profiles and Outlooks,* April, 1983.
U. S. Department of Labor. Bureau of Labor Statistics. *Monthly Labor Review,* September, 1987.
U. S. Department of Labor. Bureau of Labor Statistics, *Research Summaries,* December, 1979.
U. S. Department of Labor. Handbook of Labor Statistics, Bulletin 2175, December, 1983.
Wagschal, P. H. and Kahn, R. D. (eds.) *Fuller on education.* Amherst, MA: The University of Massachusetts Press, 1979.
Walker, R. A., Bergmann, D. The blossoming of computer aided instruction. *PC Magazine,* April 1983.
Whitman, W. *Leaves of grass.* New York: Penguin Books, 1959.
Whyte, W. H. Jr. The organization man. In Brigitte Berger editor. *Readings in Sociology.* New York: Basic Books, 1974.

Wilber, K., Editor, *Holographic paradigm and other paradoxes*. Boulder, Co.: Shambhala, 1982.

Wild Kingdom. Television show. January 16, 1983.

Wilson, L. *My career theory*. EDCO 548, Career Theory. Los Angeles: University of Southern California, Spring, 1983.

Winters, J. Addressing the fiction class at the Santa Barbara Writers Conference, June 1, 1982.

Wirth, T. *Remarks by chairman house subcommittee on telecommunications, consumer, protection, and finance*. CTM conference, Annenberg School of Communication, Los Angeles, CA: University of Southern California, 1981.

Wolf, F. A. *Taking the quantum leap: the new physics for non scientists*. New York: Harper and Row, 1981.

Zemke, R. Training in the '90s. *Training Magazine*. January, 1987.

Zukav, G. *The dancing wu li masters*. New York: William Morrow and Company, Inc., 1979.

Books on Organization

Eisenberg, Ronnie and Kelly, Kate. *Organize yourself*. New York: Macmillan, 1986.

Winston, Stephanie. *Get organized: The easy way to put your life in order*. New York: Norton, 1978.

You chose letter A

AUTHOR INDEX

You chose letter B

SUBJECT INDEX

You chose letter C

ORDER FORM

Qty	Description	Amount
_____	Book: How NOT to Make It and Succeed... ($13.95)	_____
_____	Book: LIFECAREER: The Quantum Leap into a Process Theory of Career ($7.95)	_____
_____	Booklet: LIFECAREER: How It Can Benefit You... ($4.95)	_____
_____	Newsletter: The Growing Edge: Pathways to Career Transformations - 6 issues... ($19.95, $15.00 (USA) $18.00 (outside USA) with book purchase	_____
_____	Cassette tape: Centering in Lifecareer ($8.00)	_____
	Shipping & Handling	$2.00
	Subtotal	_____
	Tax (California Residents add 7% sales tax)	_____
	Grand Total	_____

Name: _____

Address: _____

City: _____ State: _____ Zip: _____

Mail order to: **LIFECAREER Foundation
993 "C" S. Santa Fe Ave #180
Vista, CA 92083
(619) 726-6700**

ORDER FORM

Qty	Description	Amount
_____	Book: How NOT to Make It and Succeed... ($13.95)	_____
_____	Book: LIFECAREER: The Quantum Leap into a Process Theory of Career ($7.95)	_____
_____	Booklet: LIFECAREER: How It Can Benefit You... ($4.95)	_____
_____	Newsletter: The Growing Edge: Pathways to Career Transformations - 6 issues... ($19.95, $15.00 (USA) $18.00 (outside USA) with book purchase	_____
_____	Cassette tape: Centering in Lifecareer ($8.00)	_____
	Shipping & Handling	$2.00
	Subtotal	_____
	Tax (California Residents add 7% sales tax)	_____
	Grand Total	_____

Name: _____

Address: _____

City: _____ State: _____ Zip: _____

Mail order to: LIFECAREER Foundation
993 "C" S. Santa Fe Ave #180
Vista, CA 92083
(619) 726-6700

About the Author:

Anna Miller-Tiedeman, formerly Vice President of the National Institute for the Advancement of Career Education and an educator at the University of Southern California, is President of Lifecareer Foundation, Vista, California, and a recipient of the George E. Hill Distinguished Alumni Award, Ohio University. She is the author of **Lifecareer: The Quantum Leap into a Process Theory of Career, Lifecareer: How It Can Benefit You, The Individual Career Exploration,** and **The Decision-Making Organizer.** The author and her husband, Dr. David V. Tiedeman, reside in Vista, California.